"GHOSTS, TEXTS, AND EXES: SURVIVING THE ONLINE DATING CIRCUS"

BY ROCCI JACKSON

Copyright © 2025

Rocci Jackson

Paperback ISBN: 979-8-9921735-0-5
eBook ISBN: 979-8-9921735-1-2

All Rights Reserved. Any unauthorized reprint or use of this material is strictly prohibited. No part of this book may be reproduced or transmitted in any form or by any means, electronic or mechanical, including photocopying, recording, or by any information storage and retrieval system without express written permission from the author.

All reasonable attempts have been made to verify the accuracy of the information provided in this publication. Nevertheless, the author assumes no responsibility for any errors and/or omissions.

Table of Contents

Preface: Come Join the Circus (Aka, Online Dating) i

A Special Thank You v

Chapter 1 Introduction: Welcome to the Clown Show 1

Chapter 2 The Checklist Before Creating the Profile 7

Chapter 3 BEWARE of Swipe Fatigue: When It All Becomes a Blur 16

Chapter 4 The Profile Pic Lie 24

Chapter 5 Swipe Left on These Red Flags—What to Watch Out for in Dating Profiles 30

Chapter 6 Messaging: Where Conversations Go to Die 37

Chapter 7 Zero Dating: The 40-Minute Date Hack You Didn't Know You Needed 45

Chapter 8 First Date Prep: After the Zero Date, It's Time to Bring Your A-Game 53

Chapter 9 The Truth Bomb: Why You Should Share Your Secrets Before Things Get Weird 69

Chapter 10 Ghosting: The Ultimate Vanishing Act 75

Chapter 11 The Break-It-Gently Handbook: How to Say "Thanks, but No Thanks" After a Few Dates 83

Chapter 12 The Fine Art of Juggling Multiple Dates Without Dropping the Ball (or Your Sanity).. 92

Chapter 13 From Swipe Right to Sleep Tight: Moving From Casual Dating to Intimacy 101

Chapter 14 Swipe Right for Spice—The Sexual Archetypes of Dating Apps 117

Chapter 15 The Dating Dilemma—When You've Got Options and Need to Choose.. 128

Chapter 16 Success Stories: They Exist, Apparently................. 136

Chapter 17 Red Flags and Rainbows—What to Watch For in Your New Relationship... 145

Chapter 18 How to Sabotage Your New Relationship Before It Even Starts (And How to Stop) 151

Chapter 19 Surviving the Honeymoon: How to Keep the Spark Beyond Month Three 161

Chapter 20 Sharing is Caring (Except When It's Not)—Navigating Ethical Non-Monogamy Without Losing Your Mind 170

Chapter 21 Conclusion: Surviving the Dating Circus with a Grin (and a Few Memes) 178

Epilogue: The Good, The Bad, and The Totally Forgettable.... 181

Bonus Chapter 25 Ridiculous First Date Stories (When Things Went Hilariously, Horribly Wrong) 183

Preface: Come Join the Circus (Aka, Online Dating)

Well, look at you. You've made it to the preface! First of all, thanks for being here. You could be swiping right on someone who looks suspiciously like their own best man at a wedding or swiping left on someone who drinks their blood because they "like the taste." Instead, you're about to dive into this wild, weird, and hilarious ride called *online dating*.

Also, you decided to do it with a relative stranger, so that's... awkward. Unless you are my friends, family members, or current dating partners, and if so, thank you so much for your support. I truly could not ask for better people in my life. I adore you, and I do not know where I would be without you.

Anyway, I digress. We are all here to navigate dating in the digital age. So, cheers to that! (If you do not have a drink, I suggest you grab something. If you are sober, still grab something because you will get thirsty, and I have always wanted to write something that will make someone do a spit take, and I can't do that if you have a dry mouth.)

Before we begin, let's get one thing straight: this book will probably not help you find "the one." Honestly, I'm not sure there is just one person for anyone. But once I start down that path, my mother starts blushing and asking, "What is wrong with you? Who raised you?" I do believe my thoughts on non-monogamy will have to be in a second book entitled "Why Have One When You Can Have Fun: The Non-Monogamy Manifesto." So look out for Oprah's Book Club sticker on that one!

Warning: There will be multiple digressions. Ask anyone who knows me, and they'll tell you it takes me ages to finish a story.

So, strap in with your strap-on doll face. I think so much of life is interconnected, so my stories tend to be too, but I know that can be nails on a chalkboard to some people, so I will try to refrain.

Now, back to this story. It's not full of life-altering tips or scientifically-backed methods to decode someone's emoji usage. Also, if they have more emojis than words, that counts as two red flags in my book, so you should run, not walk away from that one. See, we are already getting your money's worth in this book and have not even made it to page three! Wait, you paid for this, right? You aren't that creepy person in Barnes and Noble getting your grubby little fingers on pages and then putting the book back, are you? Don't be a Kyle. (I am over people using "Karen," so it will only be known as a Kyle from now on. You are welcome; all the wonderful people out there named Karen. Let's hope this is a trend that sticks.)

Wow... That got wildly off track. I did not even make a whole page. I will try harder, I promise. If you're looking for serious advice on love, you may want to try a different section of the bookstore (or, you know, therapy—because online dating will test your patience *real* quick, and you will want to throw your phone at oncoming traffic).

But I can promise you this: by the time you've finished reading, you'll either feel a lot better about your dating life or have some pretty great stories to share at your next brunch. Either way, you win.

Why I Wrote This Book (and Why You Should Absolutely Read It)

I wrote this book because, quite frankly, I've dated a *lot*. I'm that friend who's always pushing others to go after what they want—whether it's a new job, a new hobby, or a hot date. But as much as

I love the thrill of putting myself out there, I keep bumping into single friends who are so fed up with the confusing, frustrating, can-someone-please-explain-how-this-works world of modern dating that they're ready to delete every app and adopt thirty cats instead.

So, I thought: *Hey, why not write something encouraging, poke fun at the insane drama of online matchmaking, and share some of my truly mortifying personal escapades to prove that if I can survive the dating circus, you can too?* You'll laugh, you'll cringe, and hopefully, you'll feel a little braver the next time you're swiping left on a fish-holding profile or cringing at yet another "Hey" opener.

Because if there's one thing I've learned through all the weird first dates, cringe-worthy sexts, and heroic levels of overconfidence, it's that we could all use a good laugh, a strong boundary, and an extra push to keep going when the going gets weird. And trust me, it *does* get weird.

A Few Ground Rules

Before we jump in, let's set some ground rules. Yes, online dating can be an absolute circus—full of clowns and bearded ladies (if you are into that, good for you. No shade or shame here. I just have enough of my own chin hairs, is all I am saying), tightrope walkers (the ones who try to balance seven conversations at once), and, of course, the mysterious disappearing act (aka, ghosters). But here's the deal: we're going to laugh through it, and we are going to remember that anything worthy of our time is going to take work. What else can we do when we've matched with someone whose idea of "deep conversation" is asking us our zodiac sign? Or a person who thinks they are woke because they saw the Matrix once and tells you that they would choose the blue pill because they would want to uncover the real world and not be a pawn in it.

We will embrace the awkwardness, the cringe-worthy messages, and the first dates that feel like a job interview gone wrong. And we'll remember that for every awful Tinder date, there's a great glass of wine/non-alcoholic drink waiting for us at home and a group of friends that cannot wait to hear our tale and laugh with us about the absurdity of online dating.

In Case of Emergency, Swipe Left

There may be moments while reading this book (or scrolling through dating apps) when you feel like giving up. Maybe you've just been ghosted after an entire week of texting, or maybe you've gone on yet another date where someone "forgot" to mention that their "roommates" are also their parents. It happens to the best of us.

If, at any point, you feel the urge to throw your phone or this book into the nearest body of water, I'm going to give you some very valuable advice: *Swipe left on the stress.* Take a deep breath, grab some snacks, and remind yourself that online dating is a marathon, not a sprint. (If it's a sprint, you're probably running in the wrong direction.)

And when I talk about marathons, I want you to think of binge-watching shows, not running, because that's just crazy talk. While bingeing a series, it can start slow. Sometimes, it can make you gasp, swoon, and become frustrated; you can lose some of your favorite characters and then cry because of the beautiful connections between people. So, let's get in those sweats, grab your ex's favorite hoodie (the one you swore you gave back, but it's so damn comfortable, and you were kind of a douche canoe Kevin, so I feel I am owed a severance package) and get comfortable with the uncomfortable.

A Special Thank You

Now, I'd like to take a moment to thank a few key players in this grand saga. First, I'd like to thank my phone for withstanding the emotional whiplash of being hurled onto the bed in frustration every time I received a "Hey" message at 2 a.m. or a "Miss you" after months of ghostly silence. You're a real trooper. You should be knighted, and you deserve a much sturdier case for all that I put you through regularly.

I'd also like to express my gratitude to Bumble, Tinder, Hinge, Feeld, and every other dating app that reminded me that romance is alive and well… or at least existing somewhere between "loves hiking" and "I want to wear your skin." Without you, this book would never exist, and my close friends would have much less entertainment at my expense. (Also, let's be honest, I'd have a lot more free time.)

A heartfelt *thank you* to all the wonderful, terrible, and completely forgettable people I've dated. To those who were genuinely amazing—thank you for being the sparkly unicorns in a field of mediocrity and for setting the bar so high that dating anyone after you felt like a cosmic joke of a dumpster fire. To the awful ones, I owe you a debt of gratitude for showing me exactly what I don't want and also how to set boundaries early on. Your red flags were practically neon; for that, I'm forever wiser (and quicker to end a rough date). And to the ones I barely remember? Thanks, I guess. You were probably nice, but let's be real—you were as exciting as a beige wall in an average office building, and I'd need a flowchart to keep track of who you were. Regardless of where you fall on the spectrum, you all played a part in this delightful circus, so thank you.

To my incredible friends who have not only survived but *thrived* through endless recounts of my dating misadventures—thank you from the bottom of my heart (and from the depths of my dating app). You've listened to stories about ghosting, gaslighting, and dates so bad they should come with a radioactive warning label. And yet, you stuck around, always ready to share your own tales of dating woes and triumphs, reminding me we're all in this wild ride together.

Thank you for being my sounding boards, therapists, and hype squad. Your support after each disappointing date, brutal honesty when I needed it, and endless encouragement have been everything. You're the ones who convinced me to channel my sass, misadventures, and quirky advice and turn it into something productive—like this book. Without you, I'd still be drowning in bad date stories and putting them in my weekly text chain... yes, I have a text group in which I share updates of my dating life with my closest friends and family and one ex (Shout out to Andrew who is the biggest Drama Queen in the group), instead of laughing about them here. Here's to the friendships that outlast every questionable Bumble match and to the joy of turning dating disasters into the comedic relief we all deserve.

A Big Thank You to Shawn: My Bocce Ball Dream-Catcher and Book God

Shawn, I couldn't possibly end this thank you without mentioning our "bougie" little pre-Bottle Rock bocce ball game, where I casually mentioned my wild dream of writing a book. You may have thought we were just tossing balls around, but that chat sparked the brilliance that led to this book. Little did I know, you'd be the inspiration behind so many chapters — and, more importantly, the unsung hero behind the scenes making this whole thing come to life. You've listened to every absurd story I've recounted like they were cherished gems, supported each draft of this book (even the versions that probably should never have made it past the idea board), and cheered me on like a professional hype man, even when I was convinced I'd accidentally overshare some mortifying detail (Spoiler: I did. A lot.). And then when it came time to record the audio version? You rolled up your sleeves, threw on some headphones, and somehow calmly helped me navigate my way through multiple takes and giggles. But let's be real, this book wouldn't have happened if it wasn't for your constant love, patience, and willingness to be my anchor when I'd get caught up in the chaos of it all. You're not just my partner in love, you're my partner in every "crazy" part of life, and I wouldn't change a damn thing. Thank you, Shawn, for loving me in all my unapologetically messy ways, for helping me choose the right stories (even when they made *you* question my sanity), and for being the incredibly, wonderful human you are. This book exists because you've been with me every step of the way, and I owe so much of it to you. Plus, we got to play bocce ball while I dreamed up all of this. Not a bad trade-off, if you ask me. Some people might break a sweat over a topic like this, but you've been chill as a cucumber and supportive as the best sports bra. You are comforting, secure, and always lifting me up. Here's to more bocce ball brainstorming sessions, more inside jokes, and more love that stands steady even when I'm tossing absurd new goals into the universe. I love you, you absolute rock star.

And, finally, I'd like to thank *you*—yes, you, dear reader—for joining me on this journey. Whether you're reading this while waiting for a reply to a message that's been "seen" but not answered, or you're about to head out on a date with someone who's been described as "figuring out their dating goals," I salute you. You're brave, resilient, and probably in need of a good laugh—which is exactly what this book is here for.

So, sit back, relax, and let's dive into the beautiful chaos of modern dating. Grab a drink (trust me, you're going to need it), and remember: if your date doesn't keep your attention, at least my ridiculous stories will.

Chapter 1

Introduction: Welcome to the Clown Show

Ah, online dating—the magical land where love is just a swipe away, and everyone's profile looks like they stepped out of a magazine photoshoot. Welcome to this three-ring dumpster fire, folks. It's a wild, unpredictable place full of strange creatures that will either ghost you, bombard you with memes, or ask for "more pics," even though they already have four of your best angles. Honestly, you'd think you were applying for a modeling agency instead of a date.

You've heard the success stories, right? The ones where people meet on an app and find *true love* after three cute dates, then ride off into the sunset, hand-in-hand, wearing matching sweaters? Yeah, those are about as common as unicorn sightings. For the rest of us mere mortals, online dating is like stepping into a circus—where you're both the clown and the unfortunate audience member. I hate to tell you, but you'll probably end up covered in metaphorical (or real) pie.

Speaking of being covered in metaphorical pie, my mother—a gorgeous, 60-something goddess—is now navigating life as a single woman and recently dumped a guy at a circus. Let's take a slight detour to go through this gem of a story. Picture this: it's the mid-2000s, and my mom, looking fabulous as always, agrees to a date with a guy who thought his Ed Hardy shirts were the pinnacle of fashion. Except the year is 2024, and the man is still wearing a bedazzled Ed Hardy Tiger shirt. (Clearly, red flags were already flying.) This guy, who I'll generously refer to as "Discount Romeo," had exactly two goals: impress my mom with the least effort possible and, of course, get into her pants. His grand plan?

Taking her to a circus. Because nothing says "romantic," like elephant poop and clowns with questionable intentions. Before we get to the big top fiasco, let's rewind to the "grand gesture of generosity" that Discount Romeo cooked up. On this sunny afternoon, this guy decides that he will impress my mother by making and handing out 50 turkey hot dogs to the homeless. Yes, turkey dogs. Because clearly, what says "I'm a good person" better than the world's driest, most questionable meat product slapped into a bun?

After slaving over the stove (and by "slaving," I mean microwaving them in batches), he insists my mother accompany him on his noble quest. Picture him swaggering down the street, turkey dogs in a plastic grocery bag, demanding that my mother take his picture with random unhoused folks. These folks, by the way, are giving him looks that scream, "Are you serious?" and he's posing like he's in a humanitarian magazine spread, while these poor folks are probably thinking, "Dude, even we don't want your turkey dogs." Suffice it to say, my mother was more mortified than impressed.

The circus was as budget as it gets. Think faded tents, sad cotton candy, and performers who looked like they hadn't smiled since the Reagan administration. But Discount Romeo seemed oblivious to the low-rent chaos unfolding around them. He was too busy trying to act like he wasn't on a date but a casting call for the next season of *Jersey Shore: Horny Old Man Edition*. And as if the bedazzled Ed Hardy shirt weren't enough, he spent half the night trying to drop what he thought were "smooth" lines—lines that had all the charm of a used car salesman in an Aquanet commercial.

About halfway through, as clowns tumbled in the background and an underwhelming trapeze act took center stage, Discount Romeo made his move. Not towards romance, mind you, but towards the oldest, sleaziest pitch in the book: "Wanna get out of here and go back to my place?" My mom, queen of patience and grace, smiled, patted him on the back, and said, "That won't be happening." Undeterred, he thought he would entice her into the sack with a romantic dinner at the very classy *The Old Spaghetti Factory*. Now, I'm all for some carb-loading, but this wasn't just any date. He also invited *another couple*. A group date for what was supposed to be a romantic evening? Sure, why not? The more, the messier.

So, they sit down, and everything seems okay at first. The bread's warm, the atmosphere's casual, and the other couple does their best to make small talk. My mom's date, "Discount Romeo," is already giving off some cheap vibes, but my mom, being her generous self, decides to wait and see how the evening unfolds—big mistake.

The meal progresses, and everyone's having a relatively good time—until the bill arrives. "Discount Romeo," with the confidence of a man who's clearly never been taught manners, casually pushes the check toward *my mom*, expecting her to pay. Now, let me remind you, this is a date *he* asked her on, yet here he is, expecting her to foot the bill for him and their surprise double-date guests.

But my mom? She doesn't play like that. She calmly looks at "Discount Romeo" and, with all the elegance and poise of a woman who's been through worse, says, "I won't be paying for a date you asked me on."

Cue the meltdown.

Apparently, this was not the response he was expecting. He goes from zero to "I'm not getting my way, so I'm going to throw a tantrum" in record time. He starts getting loud, causing a scene in the middle of the *Old Spaghetti Factory* as if he's auditioning for a role in the next Jerry Springer episode. The other couple? They're suddenly very interested in their pasta, trying to pretend they're not witnessing the adult equivalent of a toddler's tantrum.

And then, the pièce de résistance: when my mom—who's clearly done with his nonsense—tells him it's over, "Discount Romeo" decides that the best move is to *reverse-dump* her. That's right. He literally pouts, stomps his feet like a kid who didn't get dessert, and says, "No, *I* dumped you first!" It's as if this were some kind of emotional race, and whoever declares it first wins a prize.

At this point, my mom can barely contain her laughter. She stands up and gracefully takes her leave while he continues to sulk like a man who just realized his "show of dominance" of pushing the check backfired spectacularly.

The best part? As my mom walked away, she heard him muttering, "But I totally dumped her first," to himself, as if saying it enough times might make it true.

And just like that, Discount Romeo slunk into the night, probably wondering where it all went wrong. Spoiler: it was the Ed Hardy shirt. It is always the Ed Hardy shirt.

Moral of the story: Age does not save you from bad dates, misguided grand gestures, or men who think turkey hot dogs are the keys to your heart. It's a dating circus out there—duck when the pie's flying and never settle for a clown who thinks he's the ringmaster.

I know that was a long digression, but wasn't it worth it?

Let's be honest: nobody prepares you for the bizarre creatures lurking in this dating circus. Sure, dating apps promise fun and efficiency. Who wouldn't want to scroll through potential soulmates while eating nachos in sweatpants and watching *The Boys*? But in reality, it's more like rummaging through a flea market. You're swiping through weird, mismatched items, hoping to find something halfway decent that doesn't smell like body odor and regret. Swipe left. Swipe right. Swipe until your thumb cramps, and you start questioning your life choices.

But don't worry. I'm here to be your trusty guide through this freak show. Think of me as the sarcastic ringleader, making sure you don't fall into any traps—like thinking the "Netflix and chill" person wants to, you know, watch Netflix. Together, we'll navigate the thrilling rollercoaster of online dating: uneasy feelings when creating a profile, the strange opening line creation, the awkward silences, the weird messages, and those magical moments where you realize the person across from you is texting someone *else* under the table. Ah, romance in the digital age.

And yet… maybe, just maybe…

Despite the ridiculousness, the no-shows, and the occasional disappointment that makes you want to delete every app and move to a remote island, there's something oddly hopeful about it all. For every bad date, for every "Wait, who is this again?" moment, there is a possibility—no matter how small—that your next swipe might actually lead to something real. Crazy, right?

Maybe you'll meet someone who genuinely laughs at your weird jokes, doesn't ghost after two days, and looks like their pictures (bonus points if those pictures weren't cropped awkwardly to remove an ex). Maybe you'll even find a fellow warrior who's just as exhausted by the whole process but still willing to give it one more try.

Because, in the end, online dating is like a scavenger hunt: sure, most of what you find will be junk, but there's always a chance you'll stumble on something unexpected, something unique, something *worth* all the chaos.

So here's to the circus, my fellow daters. Who knows, you might survive—and maybe you'll come out of it with a story that doesn't end in pie to the face or a clown in your bed.

Chapter 2

The Checklist Before Creating the Profile

Before diving into the wild world of online dating, there are a few essentials you need to get in order—because online dating isn't just about swiping and hoping for the best. Think of it like as gearing up for a digital adventure; you need the right tools, mindset, and maybe a stiff drink. I want you to be prepared. I do not want you pulling a hammy before getting out of those proverbial dating racing blocks and throwing in the towel before we've even begun. So, let's warm up and stretch out. Here's what you need before starting an online dating profile:

---

1. A Sense of Humor (You'll Need It)

Let's be honest: online dating can be a hot mess. You're going to get weird messages (some with unsolicited genital photos—because let's face it, 98% of genital photos are unsolicited. By the way, genitalia? Not the most photogenic appendage. Now, send me a photo of a wenis any day… I will now wait for you to Google "wenis." You are welcome.) You'll also deal with awkward small talk, meet a few people who lie about their height, age, and weight, and encounter those who mysteriously forget to mention they're still living with their ex. The only way to survive all this madness is to laugh it off, and I cannot stress enough: write it down and share it with all of your friends. Especially the single ones! They need to know that they are not alone out there in this crazy world of online dating. We also need to encourage one another to continue to try even after tough dates. If you don't already have a solid sense of humor, develop one quickly—you'll need it to keep from throwing your phone into any body of water.

---

2. Clear Boundaries and Expectations

It is essential that you know what you're looking for *before* you start swiping. Are you here for something casual? Serious? Or do you just want to conduct a scientific experiment to see how many people think standing next to a fish in their profile picture makes them dateable? Whatever your goals are, be clear with yourself (and others) about what you're willing to entertain and what you absolutely will not. Set boundaries: what you're open to discussing, what topics are off-limits, and how quickly you're comfortable sharing personal details. Once you've set these boundaries, stick to them. Don't feel embarrassed about being honest! I have talked with so many people who get nervous and end up compromising their values or desires to please others. Don't be a politician—you are better than that. #bebetterthanapolitician.

---

3. A Solid Set of Authentic Photos (Leave the Filters at Home)

This isn't a job interview, but it's close. Your profile photos are your first impression, so make them count. Here are a few tips:

- Use recent photos. If your best pic is from five years ago, it's time to update. You want to look like yourself when you meet, not like a distant college memory.

- Ditch the heavy filters. This isn't a Snapchat or Instagram audition; you are not a Kardashian darling. You are better than that. #bebetterthanaKardashian.

- Throw in a mix—one where you're smiling, one where you're doing something you enjoy, one in a location that you love being, and maybe one where you're *not* wearing sunglasses. People need to see your eyes, not just your reflective aviators.

4. A Witty Bio (Please, No One-Worders or Novels)

The "bio" is your chance to showcase who you are beyond a nice smile and a cute dog (Although, if you have a cute dog, definitely include them. They get me every time). Keep it short, witty, and interesting. A well-crafted bio is essential because nothing says, "I'm boring," like "I like to laugh," or "Just ask." (Pro tip: Everyone likes to laugh; it's not a personality trait, and saying "just ask" makes me feel like you have something to hide and you want to eke out information slowly over time and nobody has time for that.)

If you're stuck, try including something specific, like your favorite hobby, an unusual talent, or a lighthearted fun fact about yourself. And please steer clear of bios that sound like a résumé or read like a job description—unless you're looking for a job, in which case you're on the wrong app. It is always great to ask your friends about your best qualities and how they would describe you to a potential suitor. We normally are much harder on ourselves and do not always see ourselves the way that others do. For my friends who are feeling particularly stuck in dating, I ask if I can refresh their profile. I tend to find pictures they normally would not have chosen and add things that intrigue a potential suitor. Not to toot my own horn, but "TOOT, TOOT." I am 7 out of 8 for recreating profiles and helping my friends find long-term relationships. I have one holdout: you know who you are... you will always be my problem child.

5. Patience (Lots of It)

You might think you'll find your dream person in the first few swipes, but I am sorry to say, you probably won't. Remember, online dating is a marathon, not a sprint (Again, not a running one. That is another type of crazy we will explore in my third book: "26.2 Reasons Not to Run: Why Marathons Are Just Long, Sweaty Bad Decisions.") You'll encounter a mix of great, mediocre, and downright questionable people. Some will ghost, others will send you one-word messages like "Hey," and a select few might even try to jump straight into deep conversations about your life's purpose after two exchanges. Buckle up—it will be a ride on a bull on roller skates on a rickety bridge.

6. Confidence (But Not Too Much)

Confidence is attractive, but there's a fine line between confident and cocky (Shout out to my best friend Eliza, who has been calling me Goldilocks for years because I often say that my partner needs to be "just the right amount" of things). Know your worth, but don't make your entire profile an ego trip. People respond to authenticity, so show off what makes you awesome without sounding like you're ready to start your own fan club. Confidence is knowing what you bring to the table without needing to announce it with neon Beetlejuice signs.

7. Realistic Expectations (No Giving Roses Here)

Remember, this isn't *The Bachelor*. You're not going to fall in love by the end of episode one (or date one). Some dates will be great, some will be painfully awkward, and some will make you question humanity. Set realistic expectations: you're looking for someone interesting, kind, and who (hopefully) matches their profile pictures. If sparks fly, great. If not, at least you'll have a new story to tell. Let's be real: finding a partner who's over six feet tall, rich, saves puppies, graduated from Harvard, loves their mom, *and* treats you like royalty? That's not a partner; that's a unicorn in designer shoes. While it's fun to dream about the perfect combination of model, genius, philanthropist, and dog whisperer, you might want to dial back those expectations a bit. Real people have flaws, like an annoying habit of leaving toothpaste open on the sink, an obnoxious sneeze, or a mild obsession with bad reality TV. And guess what? That's okay! You're not ordering a custom-built partner off Amazon Prime; you're meeting real, wonderful, imperfect humans. So, instead of looking for someone who checks every box on your impossible list, focus on finding someone who makes you laugh, respects you, and maybe only occasionally forgets to text back. Because trust me, "loves puppies" is great, but "willing to share their fries" might be even better.

---

8. A No-Ghost Policy (For Yourself)

It's easy to disappear on someone when things fizzle out, but don't be that person. Make a pact with yourself to avoid ghosting. If you're not feeling a connection, be upfront with a simple, "Hey, it was nice meeting you, but I don't think we're a match." It's kind, respectful, and makes the process smoother for both parties.

Ghosting is for haunted houses or while making pottery with a shirtless Patrick Swayze, not dating apps.

---

9. Thick Skin (This Is Key)

You're going to get rejected. Sometimes, it's polite, sometimes silent, and sometimes bizarre (like being unmatched mid-conversation). Don't take it personally; it's all part of the game. Develop thick skin early on, like elephant thick, because not everyone you swipe right on will swipe right on you, and that's okay. Keep your sense of self intact and move on with the grace of Michelle Obama when she had to stand next to Trump on Inauguration day (Can we all agree that this woman is the epitome of poise and grace? We all know that she wanted to knee him right in the undercarriage, but she kept it together and was a model of self-restraint. #bemorelikeMichelle.)

---

10. An Exit Strategy (Just in Case)

Not every date will go well, so it's always good to have a backup plan. Whether it's a friend calling with a fake emergency or a foolproof excuse like, "I have an early meeting tomorrow," make sure you have a way out if things take a nosedive. Trust me, you'll be grateful for it when you find yourself stuck on a date that's going south fast. It doesn't have to be something over the top. Keep it simple, keep it kind, and keep it brief.

Bonus: Treat Yo Self (Optional, but Encouraged)

Sometimes, the best way to cope with the highs and lows of online dating is by indulging in a glass of wine, hot coffee, or a favorite snack. Sometimes, we need to reward ourselves for enduring that painful conversation, the awkward side hug at the end of the date, or the stumbling, "That was uh… fun... maybe… uh…do you want to go back to..." "GOODNIGHT" conversation. It won't solve all your dating problems, but it will help you laugh them off and start to process what happened.

Story Time: Treat Yo Self Pandemic Style

Picture it: the world's on fire—metaphorically and literally, of course, thanks to COVID. Lockdowns, Tiger King, and the questionable allure of sourdough starters had us all on edge. My solution? A ladies' night at my place, complete with a social-distancing-approved seating arrangement that made us look like middle schoolers at their first dance. But we were done with the heavy stuff, the endless updates, and the boredom. It was time for something fun, frivolous, and possibly fermented.

Many of my friends and I found ourselves single during the pandemic, not really knowing what we wanted or how to even date during these tumultuous times. The plan: We'd each create a checklist detailing our ideal partner. Not just the basics—tall, dark, and handsome/gorgeous? Boring. I'm talking about the weirdly specific stuff like "Must appreciate the artistic value of 90s boy band ballads" or "Has no fear of Ikea assembly instructions." We wanted to go deep. Because if you can't be ridiculously picky during the apocalypse, when can you?

Next, to lighten the mood—and maybe lower our inhibitions—we introduced each other's checklist "dream partners" through custom cocktails. Picture a matchmaking ceremony but with bartending flair. One of my friend's dream dates became a fizzy gin concoction with a sprig of rosemary—smooth, balanced, and slightly pretentious. Another ended up with a spicy tequila nightmare that screamed, "I need a partner who likes adventure or at least can handle a fiery woman." And mine? Let's just say I unveiled what I now call an "Idris Elba." Because who embodies perfection better than Idris himself?

Let me break it down: Mr. Black Coffee Liqueur, rum, crème de banana, caramel syrup, and pineapple juice. Rich, intriguing, and unexpectedly smooth—like Idris walking onto the screen with that effortless charm. With every sip, I imagined him narrating my life, making even my sweatpants-clad existence feel cinematic.

To cap off the chaos, we made vision boards. Not the standard "dream car, dream house" kind—oh no, these were boards dedicated to the Hallmark-movie-worthy star who'd portray our perfect partner. A pine-log cabin, a golden retriever, maybe a flannel shirt or two. My board looked like Idris Elba wandered into a Christmas village, saved my struggling bakery, and decided to stay forever.

And for a few glorious hours, we forgot the world was unraveling outside. We laughed about impossible standards, toasted to unrealistic Hallmark scenarios, and convinced ourselves that maybe, just maybe, the Idris Elba of cocktails and criteria wasn't too much to ask for—pandemic or not.

Now that you're fully equipped—armed with humor, honest boundaries, and a willingness to embrace the awkward—you're ready to venture into the wild world of online dating. So go forth, conquer this digital dating jungle, and remember: the right person will appreciate you for exactly who you are. Armed with wit, charm, and a rock-solid sense of humor, you might just find someone who's delightfully weird in all the right ways—just like you. If not, well, you've got enough material for a best-selling memoir and a stand-up routine. Win-win.

Chapter 3
BEWARE of Swipe Fatigue:
When It All Becomes a Blur

There's something magical about the first few days of being on a dating app. The possibilities seem endless—so many faces, so many potential connections. You feel a rush of excitement and optimism, giddy with the idea of finding "the one" as you swipe right on profile after profile, imagining your future with each new match. Maybe this one likes the same Apple TV shows as you. Maybe that one is into Comic-Con and will dress up as Sailor Moon with you. So much potential!

But then, after a few weeks (or, let's be real, a few hours), the thrill starts to fade. Swipe left, swipe right, swipe until your thumb feels like it's going to fall off, and suddenly, every profile looks the same. You can no longer distinguish between "Loves long walks on the beach" and "Looking for someone to join my doomsday cult." You've hit **Swipe Fatigue**, and the magic is gone.

The Swiping Zombie

You start with intention, carefully reading bios, checking photos, and thinking about whether you'd connect with someone. But as Swipe Fatigue sets in, your standards become a blurry mess of "Sure, why not?" and "Wait, who was that again?"

It's like swiping on autopilot. You're not looking at the profiles anymore; you're just swiping because that's what you're supposed to do. And then you catch yourself swiping right on someone whose bio says, "Looking for a woman to help me raise my bee colonies," and you stop to wonder, "How did I get here?"

It's like you've turned into a swiping zombie, mindlessly moving your thumb without actually engaging with anything. Who needs brains when you've got endless profiles to shuffle through?

Profiles Start to Blur

After a while, all the profiles start to look the same. Everyone "loves adventure" is "looking for someone who can make them laugh" and has a photo of them holding a cocktail on a rooftop. Is this one person with multiple accounts, or have you just been swiping for too long? Are all these dating profiles *generated* in the same factory?

It's like some universal dating app template was handed out to everyone, and they all filled in the same details. If I see one more person who's "really good at trivia" and "obsessed with tacos," I might throw my phone out the window. Tacos are great, but let's be real—tacos won't keep this relationship going (although, if you surprise your partner with tacos often, I can almost guarantee it will help you stay together).

The Bio Mystery: Decoding the Hieroglyphics

Speaking of bios, let's talk about the masterpieces that range from one-word answers to cryptic messages that require a secret decoder ring. Some people put *way* too much info, listing every single interest they've ever had (Do I really need to know you're "kinda into stamp collecting, but only on Sundays?"), while others just drop a single word like "Adventurous."

"Adventurous" in what sense? Are we talking about spontaneous road trips or surviving a weekend in the wilderness with nothing but a granola bar and a dream? Some clarity would be nice, but you're left swiping based on half a sentence and a blurry photo.

And don't get me started on the people who just use emojis. What am I supposed to do with 🍕🏋️✈️? Am I supposed to infer that you like pizza, working out, and traveling? Or is this a coded message about your plans for world domination, starting with a pizza-themed gym franchise? I can't tell, and I am too exhausted to figure it out.

The Emoji Apocalypse

But the real test of your sanity comes when you encounter **The Emoji Bio.** Someone out there decided it would be "cute" or "whimsical" to convey their entire personality via tiny pictures. Instead of words, you get a chaotic collage of wine glasses, airplanes, flexed biceps, cats, cacti, and maybe a random avocado. Now you're sitting there like a modern-day archaeologist, squinting at your phone and trying to interpret this digital Rosetta Stone. What does the cactus next to the martini mean? Are they a prickly alcoholic? Are they warning you they're as dry as the desert but still want to party? Should you pack a first-aid kit if you date them?

Your mind spirals. The airplane could mean they travel a lot, or maybe they just love those in-flight pretzels. The cat emoji might mean they're a proud cat parent—or perhaps they're allergic, and the cat is their spirit animal mocking them daily. The flexed biceps might imply they're a gym rat, or maybe it's their way of saying they're strong enough to carry your emotional baggage. Without words, it's all guesswork.

Before you know it, you've spent more time trying to decode this profile than you'd ever admit. Are they international jet-setters who enjoy workout classes, sipping martinis in the desert, and cuddling exotic pets? Or are they just messing with you? By the time you "figure it out" (spoiler: you never really do), you've either swiped left out of frustration or, worse, swiped right out of sheer curiosity—setting yourself up for a first date you'll need to decode in real-time.

Because that's the beauty of the emoji apocalypse: it reminds you that in the world of online dating, words are overrated, logic is scarce, and you'll always wonder if the cactus-and-martini combo was a secret red flag all along.

Swipe Regret: The "Oops, I Swiped Right on That?" Moment

Once Swipe Fatigue sets in, you're bound to have some **Swipe Regret**. You wake up the next morning, check your matches, and suddenly realize you swiped right on someone who looks like they live in a bunker and collect medieval weaponry. Or maybe you matched with someone whose entire bio is in Comic Sans and boldly declares, "I'm the real deal."

And let's not forget the times you swipe out of sheer boredom and immediately regret it. You're just swiping away, not paying attention, and then *whoops*, you accidentally matched with someone with a profile picture of themselves wearing a snake as a scarf. Now, you're stuck in a conversation with them about their reptile collection.

It's like online dating is out to remind you that your poor decisions don't disappear—they match with you and start asking, "What's up?"

Swipe Math: The Odds Are (Definitely) Not in Your Favor

Let's do some dating app arithmetic, shall we? Say you swipe right on 100 profiles. Out of those, let's generously assume 10 people swipe right on you in return. Pause for a quick round of self-high-fives—you've got some game, apparently. But out of those 10 magical matches, maybe 3 will actually break the silence and message you. (And by "message," I mean something beyond a rogue emoji or the world's laziest "Hey.")

Now, from those 3 brave souls who dared to start a conversation, maybe—just maybe—1 will surpass the thrilling "So how's your day?" phase. That's right, just one potential superstar who can actually converse like a normal human being rather than treating the chat like they're waiting for your cue in a high-stakes improv scene. If fate is feeling extra generous, that unicorn of a human might actually meet you in person. Yes, real-life, three-dimensional, possibly wearing pants.

These numbers are about as encouraging as the prospect of the Las Vegas Raiders winning the Super Bowl. It's like playing the lottery, where the grand prize is a semi-decent date who doesn't make you question all your life choices. After swiping through a few hundred profiles, you might downgrade your hopes from "The One True Love" to "The One Who Knows How to Use Full Sentences." Because hey, at this point, literacy is sexy.

But here's the twist: while the odds sound bleaker than a rom-com marathon on a rainy day, consider each swipe an adventure. Sure, it's a treasure hunt where most "treasure" turns out to be rusty bottle caps, but every so often, you stumble upon something shiny—a conversation that clicks, a shared joke that actually makes you laugh out loud instead of rolling your eyes in frustration.

So keep swiping, my friend. Embrace the ridiculousness and treat it like a bizarre carnival game. Sometimes, the best you can do is aim, throw, and hope to pop that balloon. Who knows? You might just win a giant plush teddy bear that you have no use for (a.k.a. a decent date). And if not, at least you'll have some killer stories to share at brunch, where everyone will toast to your efforts and refill your mimosa.

Burnout Mode: When You Just Can't Anymore

Eventually, the swiping gets to you. You hit **Burnout Mode**. You can't even muster the energy to open the app anymore. Every notification feels like a chore. You get a message from someone, and instead of being excited, your first thought is, "Ugh, now I have to respond and pretend I am interested in their trip to Yosemite."

Swipe Fatigue makes you start to question the entire system. "Is this really how people find love now? Am I going to meet my soulmate by swiping right on a picture of someone dressed in an adult onesie?"

You start fantasizing about a world where dating apps don't exist, where people meet in coffee shops or bookstores or by bumping into them on the busy streets of Manhattan like they do in the movies. But here you are, back in reality, swiping through profiles that all blur together in one endless loop.

Story Time: Swipe Fatigue Gone Wrong

Let me tell you about when I swiped right on someone out of pure swipe exhaustion. It had been a long day. I'd swiped through what felt like a hundred profiles, and my brain was officially in zombie mode—no more reading bios. No more carefully inspecting photos. Just pure, mindless swiping.

So there I was, in full autopilot mode, swiping right on someone who, at first glance, seemed normal enough. They had a nice smile and seemed into hiking, and their bio mentioned something about loving animals. Seemed harmless, right? WRONG.

The next morning, I woke up to find a new message from my match. I opened it up and was immediately greeted with the words: "You are beautiful. I like to be pretty upfront, and I think aliens built the pyramids, which will be something that we will talk about on our first date." Oh no. I swiped right on a conspiracy theorist. My finger had betrayed me.

Naturally, my first thought was that they must be joking, but I decided to check out their profile again to see if there were any red flags I had missed the first time. And that's when I noticed the second part of their bio (which I had completely glazed over in my swipe fatigue haze). It said, "Looking for someone to join me on my quest to uncover the secrets of the Illuminati." I had swiped right on someone who believed they were the Indiana Jones of conspiracy theories, and I am not trying to be anyone's Short Round.

Now, I was faced with a dilemma: do I unmatch immediately, or do I lean into the madness and ask their thoughts on crop circles? In the end, I opted for the polite, "I don't think we're a good match," and swiftly exited the conversation. But that experience taught me one very important lesson: never swipe when you're on dating app autopilot.

Optimistic End Note

But here's the thing—swipe fatigue is temporary. Sometimes, you need to take a break, log out, and remind yourself that online dating is supposed to be *fun*. The endless swiping can make it feel like a never-ending buffet of bios, emojis, and profile pics, but when you least expect it, that one person who stands out from the crowd will pop up. And suddenly, the fatigue will melt away, replaced with the excitement of possibility.

So, don't let swipe fatigue get you down. Take a deep breath, grab a snack, and swipe on. You never know—your next swipe could be the one that makes all this craziness worth it.

Chapter 4
The Profile Pic Lie

Now that you have been warned that swiping can be work let's start with some of the basics of looking at a profile. The profile picture is the window to the soul... or at least, to who you *wish* you were. Let's be real: the profile pic is the foundation of your entire online dating experience. And yet, it's also the stage where the biggest lies are told. It's like the Photoshop Hunger Games, and guess what? We all volunteered as tribute.

There's nothing quite like the anticipation of meeting someone for the first time, armed only with the knowledge of their carefully curated images. You know the ones—perfect lighting, flattering angles, possibly a filter strong enough to disguise even Bigfoot as a runaway bride. Then you meet them in person and immediately wonder, "Did they send their father in their place to vet me? Was there a time machine involved?" Let's take some time to walk through the photos that make most want to scream, "WTF?"

The "Group Photo" Gamble

The group photo is one of the greatest crimes in the world of profile pictures. You're scrolling, minding your business, when suddenly, you're presented with a picture of *five people* laughing at a wedding. It's like dating roulette—who am I supposed to be attracted to here? The tall person in the middle? The friend who's clearly had one too many? Or, my personal favorite, the person wearing the huge hat who looks more like a prop than a participant?

Nothing says "I'm confident in who I am," like forcing your potential date to play Sherlock Holmes to figure out which one of the crew you actually are. Pro tip: if it takes more than three swipes to locate you, we're moving on. Also, if I must play "Guess Who?" with your photos, I'm half-expecting to swipe right and be matched with the person I hoped you *weren't*.

The "I think I am Bear Grylls" Pic.

If their profile looks like an audition for *Survivor*—complete with fishing, hiking, skiing, and possibly wrestling a bear—it's time to pause. Sure, we all like fresh air, but when every picture is an action shot in the wilderness, it starts to feel intimidating and unrealistic. Are we going on dates, or are you about to make me summit a mountain on the first date or fish in a river with full waders on? It paints them as a bit one-dimensional—like the only thing they know how to do is tie knots and pose with a fish. Where's the balance? It's great that you love the outdoors, but I need to know if you also have the range to, you know, sit on a couch and watch a movie sometimes or go out to eat without having to catch our dinner first.

The "I Am Constantly Going to A Themed Party Pic."

Oh, great—you're fun, adventurous, and love a theme. I'm all for someone who can throw on a costume and live it up at a toga party or '70s night. But when every photo is you dressed as a pirate, an '80s rocker, or a guy from the Village People, I start to wonder if I'll be roped into some annual Elvis look-a-like competition in Tempe, Arizona. Nothing says "hard pass" like imagining myself in a sparkly jumpsuit next to an Elvis wannabe under that unrelenting sun next to lizard people. One themed photo? Cute. Seven? I'm packing my bags and heading for the hills.

The "10 Years Ago" Pic

Then there's the **crowd from 10 years ago**. These brave souls seem to have forgotten that time exists. You swipe right on a chiseled jawline, a full head of hair, and the spark of youth in their eyes, only to show up and discover they've brought their dad's face, grandpa's hairline, and bulldog's jawline.

Seriously, how do they think this is going to go down? Sure, in 2010, you were probably living your best life—wearing bootcut jeans, drinking vodka Red Bulls, and belting out "Like a G6" at the club. But this is 2024. We've all been through some stuff, and if your profile pic still features a Blackberry, we need to talk.

And don't even get me started on those who have clearly lost a fight with gravity but are still holding on to the fantasy. Look, we've all aged—just embrace it. Pretending your photos aren't older than the average Senate member is rude. This was supposed to be a flirtatious interaction, not a game of spot the decade your picture belongs to. #weneedtermlimitsonourrepresentatives #75yearoldwealthywhiteguysdon'tunderstandaverageamericanproblems.

The Sunglasses and Hat Brigade

Then there's the person who rocks sunglasses in *every* photo. You know the type—they're out at the beach, standing on a mountain, or driving a convertible, and not once do you see their actual face. It's like they're in the witness protection program for eyeballs. The first time you meet them without the shades? Surprise! Their eyes are either tiny dots you didn't see coming or so wildly cross-eyed you're not sure if they're looking at you or a squirrel across the street.

And hats. Why is everyone in a hat? What are you hiding under there? Hairline problems? A rogue bird? I swear, if you can't show me your uncovered head in at least *one* photo, I'm going to assume the worst—that you've been bald since you were 19, or your fashion sense is that of "frat boy circa 2005."

The Professional Photographer Shots

Let's chat for a second about the people who hire professional photographers for their profile pics. Calm down; this isn't a modeling audition for Calvin Klein, complete with moody lighting, artfully tousled hair, and that "casual" lean against a luxury car. One professional pic can be nice, but when every single shot is retouched and curated by the gods, it starts to feel like I'm swiping on someone's Acting CV. It's giving "I don't get out of bed for less than $10k," which, let's be real, is *terrifying*. And here's the kicker: no one has real-life touch-up software (Except maybe that weirdo Elon Musk, who is a Cyborg with American Girl Doll coloring). If I need to hire a photographer to keep up, it's a swipe left for me.

Story Time: Catfish: GQ Edition.

Now, let me tell you about the time I got catfished. If I am being honest, I have been catfished more times than I would like to admit. I have been catfished by all genders and ages, and it does not get easier. Anyways, I matched with someone who had the most stunning photos—like, this person looked like they just walked off a red carpet. They had this killer smile and perfect hair and seemed genuinely fun based on their bio. I was looking forward to seeing this stunner in person and was hopeful that we would connect.

Fast forward to the day we meet up. I arrive at the coffee shop, scanning the room for the gorgeous human who had practically *charmed* my pants right off through my phone screen. And there, at a corner table, sat… a very different version of my match. I'm talking about someone whose profile pics must have been taken during the Great Gatsby era because they looked like they had aged about thirty years since those shots.

I approached cautiously, and as I got closer, I thought, "Maybe they just had a rough day?" But then I saw the unkempt hair, the oversized T-shirt that literally read, "World's Okayest Person," and the undeniable scent of desperation and mothballs. I spent the entire coffee date trying to remember if there had been any red flags I missed, like a mention of "I have a 1980s haircut" or "I voted for Regan back in college."

By the end of our conversation, I realized I had been duped, and all I could think was, "Well, at least I can tell my friends a time traveler catfished me."

The Reality Check

Look, I get it. We all want to put our best foot forward. But if your profile pic and real-life appearance are distant cousins at best, we have a problem. Newsflash: if you look nothing like your photos, there's no way this ends well. I'm going to show up and be more shocked and frustrated than excited. I signed up to meet the person from that profile picture, not their much older, less photogenic relative.

And this isn't just about any one gender! Let's not pretend everyone doesn't pull this trick. Between the filters, the angles, and the strategic lighting, we've all committed a few profile photo sins. But remember: there's a fine line between enhancing our features and flat-out lying. If your date is scanning the bar for the person in your photos and walks right past you… that's a problem.

So, here's a revolutionary concept: *just look like yourself.* I know it's radical, but trust me, it'll pay off. Instead of the "Oh wow, you look *different*" conversation (which is never good), how about we aim for "Wow, you look even better in person!" I promise it's less awkward that way.

Optimistic End Note

And believe it or not, there's a silver lining. While profile pic lies are frustrating, some people *do* look like their photos—some even look better in real life (I know, it's shocking). So, keep swiping. Every now and then, you'll meet someone who's refreshingly honest, and you'll feel like you've won the online dating lottery.

So, good luck, brave dater. May your matches be real, your photos be accurate, and your sunglasses removed at least once.

Chapter 5

Swipe Left on These Red Flags—What to Watch Out for in Dating Profiles

Let's face it: the dating pool isn't just filled with fish—it's a chaotic aquarium teeming with bizarre, cringe-worthy, and sometimes confusing creatures. While some species are harmless (and maybe even fun to date), others should come with a warning label. Here's a guide to the ones you want to look out for:

1. The "Just Here for a Good Time" Chameleon
Profile Bio: "Not looking for anything serious. Just seeing where things go."

They're not here for a relationship but for a temporary distraction. Depending on what you're after, this person changes their intentions like a mood ring. If you're looking for commitment, they'll mysteriously vanish right after you suggest getting brunch next week. If you're into casual fun, suddenly they're talking about meeting your family. They're the ultimate shapeshifter, but not in a fun, superhero way—more like a confusing, *"What do you even want?"* way. Be wary of these slippery creatures. The more you try to understand or decipher their messages, the more elusive they become. Sure, you're up for adventure, but dating the Davinci Code wasn't what you signed up for.

2. The Emoji Enthusiast
Profile Bio: 🌍🍕✌️👽

Do you speak fluent emoji? No? Well, neither do the rest of us. This person has decided that instead of using words like the rest of society, they will communicate exclusively through tiny icons that only vaguely hint at their personality. You'll spend more time deciphering their cryptic combinations (why is there a pizza next to a globe, and is that a peace sign or the shocker?) than actually getting to know them. Unless you're prepared for entire conversations made of faces and fruit, swipe left.

---

3. The "Still in the Friend Zone with My Ex" Person
Profile Bio: "My ex and I are still really good friends, but we're totally over each other, I swear!"

You know what's fun? Being constantly compared to someone's ex while they insist they're "just friends." This person comes with *all* the baggage and none of the closure. You'll be on a date, and guess who keeps texting? You guessed it, the ex. They'll spend half the time telling you how their ex still comes over to "hang out as friends" and the other half convincing you that they have moved on. Spoiler alert: they haven't.

Having a healthy relationship with an ex? Great, that's a sign of maturity. It means they won't pull a "Left Eye" Lopes (RIP—if you don't know TLC, please pause the reading of this book and look them up) and set their shoes on fire in the bathtub. It's almost a green flag—*almost*. But when every conversation starts with, "Oh, my ex always used to…" or "Funny, my ex and I did that too," it's less about maturity and more like they've brought a plus-one to your date... an invisible one, but still. It's one thing to be on good terms; it's another to be so connected that their ex is practically living rent-free in their head. And if that's the case? It might be time to gracefully exit before you become an unwilling part of this awkward, unwanted love triangle.

4. The "I'm So Nice" Serial Proclaimer

Profile Bio: "I'm a really nice person! Just looking for someone who won't play games."

Let's be real: If you have to advertise your niceness like it's on clearance, it probably isn't flying off the shelves. This person spends more time proclaiming their kindness than actually practicing it. They'll tell you how they're always getting "friend-zoned" or "used," and somehow it's someone else's fault—usually blaming everyone and everything for being single. Brace yourself for the inevitable nice guy/gal/person rant when things don't go their way; they'll make sure you know that "people like you" just don't appreciate genuine kindness. Spoiler alert: genuine kindness doesn't come with a side of guilt.

5. The Mysterious Traveler
Profile Bio: "Always on the go! Just got back from hiking the Andes and headed to Tokyo next week."

Sounds exciting, right? Until you realize that they probably will not be in the same zip code long enough for you to learn their last name. Sure, their profile is full of cool travel pics (which could easily be stock photos), but good luck meeting them. They'll regale you with stories about their *many* adventures and tell you they can't wait to share them with you while simultaneously scheduling flights, leaving you wondering whether you just dated an actual human or a flight itinerary.

6. The "All I Do is Work" Hustler

Profile Bio: "I'm super focused on my career, but I'm open to making time for the right person!"

Ah, yes, the elusive workaholic. Dating them feels like trying to schedule a meeting with a busy CEO—they're always on the clock. Their calendar is jam-packed with important things like "working lunches," "business trips," and *"late meetings,"* so you'll always come second to their work email and phone calls. They might text you here or there—usually during their 15-minute coffee break or walks to the copier—but if you're hoping for more than a Zoom call between their work projects, good luck.

7. The Philosopher Who Never Stops Talking

Profile Bio: "Let's get deep. I'm all about intellectual conversations. What's your stance on the meaning of life?"

Prepare for every conversation to feel like you're taking the SATs. This person can't just chat about casual topics like their favorite show or hometown quirks. Instead, they'll hit you with *"What does it all mean?"* during what you thought was a casual dinner. You'll be trying to enjoy a glass of wine, and they'll dive deep into existentialism, wondering aloud if love is just a social construct created by capitalism. Unless you're in the mood for a TED Talk where you are the only audience member, proceed with caution.

8. The Gym Selfie King/Queen

Profile Bio: "I'm all about fitness. Swipe if you can keep up with my gains!"

Oh, you've never seen someone in the gym before? Well, lucky for you, this person will show you *every* angle of their workout routine. Their entire gallery consists of sweaty mirror selfies, flexing in front of gym equipment, and the occasional "cheat meal" pic of a chocolate protein shake. If you love lifting weights, it's great! If not, prepare for conversations that revolve around meal prepping, counting macros, and how they're on their fifth "bulking session" this year. Swipe left unless you're ready to date someone whose main relationship is with their biceps and grams of protein.

---

9. The Spiritual Guru

Profile Bio: "Aligning my chakras. Seeking a twin flame."

This person's energy is *literally* the most important thing in the universe—and yours better be, too. They'll ask for your birth chart before even learning your last name, and if your rising sign doesn't match theirs, it's game over. Expect frequent conversations about energy healing, crystal grids, and that one amazing spiritual journey they took on ayahuasca in Tulum. They might be the calm, positive influence you need—or they'll suggest cleansing your aura after one too many drinks of hard Kombucha.

10. The One With "No Drama" But Actually Has All the Drama

Profile Bio: "Looking for someone with no drama. No crazies."

Don't you love the person who repeatedly tells you that they "do not do drama." The irony? They're the most dramatic person you'll ever meet. They claim to avoid drama, but their entire life is an episode of *The Real Housewives*. They'll tell you how everyone they've dated was "so much drama" and then create a soap opera out of everything. You'll get roped into arguments over who left the salt shaker in the wrong spot or why the barista didn't get their coffee hot enough. They tend to find a reason to complain about anything and everything and have the emotional maturity of a toddler who has a full diaper and has missed nap time. Be ready for over-the-top reactions to the smallest things.

Story Time: A Night at the Oscars

I once dated this guy who could've won an Oscar for "Best Performance in a Never-Ending Crisis." He was smart, funny, and attractive (the trifecta!), so I thought I'd hit the dating jackpot. But it turned out I'd merely opened a Pandora's box of soap opera-level drama. You name it, he was facing it. His boss allegedly had it out for him, his landlord was deliberately ignoring repairs just to spite him, his car got hit in a gym parking lot by some phantom driver who vanished into the night, and he supposedly had a stalker who refused to back off—so much so, that he claimed he had to get a restraining order. At first, I was like, "Wow, what terrible luck!" and offered my best empathetic head-tilts and "Oh, that's so awful" consolations.

But after a while, I started to think: *No one is this unlucky.* Not even Wilmer McLean, the guy whose land was caught between both Union and Confederate forces during the Civil War, is that unlucky. You didn't think there would be random historical facts in this book, did you? I'm full of surprises!

So, I put on my amateur detective hat and started to sniff out the truth. Turns out, his boss "hated" him because he wasn't actually doing his job—he was dumping his workload onto his coworkers like an unwanted fruitcake at Christmas. His landlord wasn't ignoring repairs out of spite but because he was three months behind on rent and avoiding calls. And that "stalker" he couldn't shake? Yeah, that was actually his wife—the mother of his child—trying to track him down because he was apparently breaking more promises than a politician after they get elected. The restraining order? Let's just say the story didn't quite match up once I dug deeper.

When the pieces fell into place, I didn't stick around for the season finale. I got myself out of that fiasco faster than my dog fleeing a vacuum cleaner. The moral of the story: trust your gut. If someone's life story sounds more dramatic than a telenovela, don't be afraid to question it. Because let's face it, no one's luck is that consistently terrible… unless they're the cause.

Navigating the wild world of online dating can feel like a full-time job, but at least you're armed with this guide to help you avoid some of the more questionable characters. Stay alert, stay witty, and when in doubt—swipe left.

Chapter 6

Messaging: Where Conversations Go to Die

So, you've swiped right, and they have swiped right too. Congratulations! You've officially entered the second circle of online dating hell: messaging. This is where things get spicy—or, more often than not, where they fizzle out faster than a cheap firework on the 5th of July. You're here to flirt, banter, and maybe even tease a little… but instead, you're getting hit with the dreaded "Hey."

Ah, yes, the one-word opener. Nothing says, "I'm ready to sweep you off your feet," like the least amount of effort humanly possible. It's the messaging equivalent of lying there like a starfish expecting a *50 Shades of Grey* experience. So sexy, right? Here's a hot tip: if the conversation opener is something you could text your grandma, you're doing it wrong.

Here are some types of communicators you may run into on your dating journey:

The Over-Confident Flirt

This person swings for the fences right out of the gate with the "So… what are you wearing?" message. We've all met this wannabe Casanova who thinks their opening line should be bold, seductive, and dripping with innuendo. Instead of igniting a spark, it's like being doused with cold water. Calm down, Romeo. It's 9 a.m. I'm still eating cereal in my pajamas. Let's not start with sexy talk before I've even had my coffee.

Honestly, what's the rush? Slow down! Messaging is the foreplay of online dating, the build-up before you meet in person. You wouldn't skip straight to dessert before having dinner, so why jump right into the steamy stuff before you've even had a basic chat about hobbies? Okay, stop. That sentence was ridiculous. Of course, you want to have dessert first, and you should do that often. Let's replace that with putting your shoes on before your pants—not the best look unless you're aiming for a serious fashion statement. Don't get me wrong; a little flirty banter is always welcome—just try to make it at least mildly clever. If you lead with, "How naughty are you?" I can only assume you've just googled "sexy things to say in 5 words or less."

The Over Texter

"What's that sound?" The over-texter—a walking notification ding. It starts innocently enough with a "Good morning, beautiful" at 7:03 a.m., and before you've even had your coffee, they've already checked in twice to see how your morning is going. By lunch, it's a barrage of "hope you're having a great day" messages, and by dinner, they're sending you a play-by-play of their last pickleball match and ending the night with a very ominous "thinking of you." Making you feel like you may be messaging Buffalo Bill, and he is about to ask you to put the lotion on the skin. You can't even exhale without a *ding*. And you know, deep down, if they're like this now, it will only get *worse* once you're exclusive. Because apparently, breathing without their hourly check-in is not a part of the relationship package.

The Copy and Paster

Copy and paste is great for addresses and phone numbers, don't get me wrong, but dating messages? C'MON MAN! You know the type—their messages have all the charm of an email newsletter you never subscribed to. They ignore your questions entirely, then hit you with generic icebreakers like, "So, what do you do for fun?" even though your profile literally says you love hiking, reading, and travel. You can practically feel the Ctrl+C Ctrl+V energy radiating from their messages. It's like they've got one conversation script saved in a Word doc, and they're just sprinkling it around the internet, hoping someone bites. Look, I get it—we're all busy. But if I wanted a pre-recorded message, I'd call customer service.

The Endless Emoji Flirt

Can we talk about the person who thinks sending a string of winking emojis counts as flirting? I'm sorry, but a wink, followed by three fire emojis and a peach, isn't giving me butterflies. It's giving me fruit salad at a BBQ vibe. Are we flirting or grocery shopping?

It's like they're trying to initiate a sexting session using nothing but hieroglyphics. You've got eggplants flying left and right, and you're sitting there like, "What's next, a tractor? A dragon? What are we doing here?" Sexy texting requires actual *words*—not an entire farmers market. At the very least, if you're going to go down the emoji route, throw in something clever. I don't know, maybe a taco next to a piña colada. We can pretend that's a cute date idea instead of just my shopping list for Whole Foods.

The "Poet"

Now, for every minimalist texter out there, you've got the **poet**. You know the type: their messages read like something from a cheap romance novel. They'll send you an essay on how the moon reminds them of your eyes and how your presence is like a summer breeze. And you're sitting there thinking, "It's been three messages; calm down, Keats. I just asked what your favorite TV show is."

While I appreciate the effort, there's something a little unsettling about being compared to the stars and the sea by someone who still calls their mom for laundry tips. Thanks, but let's dial back the *Wuthering Heights* vibe until after we've met for at least a drink. Sexy talk is great, but you're missing the mark if I have to re-read your message three times to figure out if you're flirting or writing an AP Lit essay.

The Disappearing Act

And then there's the classic: things are heating up, you're vibing, and just when the conversation's getting good, poof—they vanish. No explanation, no goodbye, just… radio silence. Were we not just exchanging some sultry messages? Did they fall into a texting black hole? Did their phone spontaneously combust from the sexual tension?

Whatever the case, it's a total vibe killer. You can practically feel the tumbleweeds rolling through your chat as you wait for a response that never comes. I imagine these people like seductive spies, sliding into your DMs with charm and innuendo, only to disappear on their next covert mission to flirt with someone else. Sure, I was ready to discuss my favorite musical artist. But now? I'm just left with unanswered questions and half-written replies.

When Sexy Turns Awkward

Of course, the real danger in sexy messaging is when it backfires. You're trying to keep things light, playful, and a little sultry. You throw out a coy line like, "I guess you'll have to wait and see…" and immediately, your match responds with something completely… *wrong*.

"Wait and see what?" "Oooh… you planned a surprise for me?" Oh, no. Abort mission. They missed the vibe. You were flirting, and they think you are hinting at some sort of kink. Suddenly, you're left standing in the ashes of what was supposed to be a sexy exchange, awkwardly explaining that you weren't, in fact, bringing whips and chains to your date to Dave and Busters.

We've covered all the ways texting can go horribly wrong—now, let's talk about how to make it go gloriously right.

1. Ditch the Snooze-Fest Opener

If you start with "How are you?" or "What's up?" you've already lost my attention. Sure, it's polite, but it's about as memorable as the sample soap at a motel. Instead, aim for an opener that sparks curiosity or laughter. I like to ask a question of the day—something that helps me understand their values, interests, or thoughts on the world.

Example:
"Quick question: if you could live in any fictional world—Hogwarts, Middle-earth, or The Marvel Universe—where are you going, and what's the first thing you do?"

Boom. You've just differentiated yourself from the 87 "What are you doing?" messages they've seen that day.

---

2. Match Their Messaging Style

Not everyone has the bandwidth (or interest) to text all day, especially if they're dealing with, you know, real life. If they send you just a few messages throughout their workday, don't flood their inbox with a never-ending stream of texts. Instead, match that pace. Conversely, if you're the one who's swamped, let them know. A simple note like, "Hey, work's crazy today—I'll reply in chunks, but I'm really interested in our convo," shows you respect their time and your own boundaries. It also makes you look thoughtful and considerate.

3. Add Some Multimedia Magic

Reading line after line of text can get stale fast. Mix it up with pictures or voice notes. If you're on a hike, send a snap of that breathtaking view. If you have a sultry or energetic voice, consider dropping a quick voice message—maybe answering the day's big question so they can hear your intonation. Texting can be so one-dimensional; adding a different sense to the mix keeps things fresh and more personal.

4. Do Your Homework: Curiosity for the Win

If they mention they're into an artist named Myles Smith (he's amazing, go check him out), take five minutes to find a track on Spotify and share your thoughts. If they play real-life Quidditch, ask if they're a Chaser or a Beater. Showing genuine interest in their hobbies (even if they're out of left field) can turn a casual chat into something deeper. Effort stands out like a neon sign in a sea of "K, cool, haha" responses.

Pro Tip: Set reminders. If they mention an event they're anxious about—a big test, a pet's surgery, or a press conference (more on that soon)—jot it down. Nothing says "I care" like remembering and following up later.

5. The "Shawn" Moment: Effort in Action

True story: I once mentioned to a guy, let's call him Shawn because that is his name, and you will be hearing a lot about him later, that I'd be speaking at a press conference with the Attorney General. Even though Shawn and I had only been talking for a few weeks, I shared with him that I was nervous about the event because it meant a lot to me and the work that I do. On the day of the event, he not only sent me a text wishing me luck but also found the livestream link on the AG's website. He watched my entire speech and later messaged me with supportive feedback—like which lines he found most moving. That level of attention and effort blew me away. Effort is everything, folks.

6. Show Genuine Interest (Yes, People Can Tell)

Lobbing a great question their way is step one. Actually reading and responding to their answer is step two. Authentic curiosity means you're paying attention, asking follow-ups, and letting the conversation unfold organically rather than firing off random questions like a robot on autopilot.

7. Close the Conversation Gracefully

Know when to wrap it up. Maybe you're off to bed, or the show you've been binge-watching just dropped a new episode. A thoughtful sign-off like, "Gotta go, genuinely enjoyed talking with you—can't wait to pick up where we left off!" leaves them excited for the next chat rather than abruptly ghosting mid-question.

Final Takeaways

- **Be Original:** No more "How r u?" Let your message stand out from the deluge of mediocre openings.

- **Match Their Energy:** Mirror their frequency and style to avoid overwhelming or underwhelming them.

- **Spice It Up:** Pics, voice notes, or day-to-day glimpses of your life keep the conversation lively.

- **Stay Curious:** Delve into their interests. Show them you actually care about their passions, no matter how niche.

- **Make an Effort:** Small gestures—like remembering their event or big day—earn big points.

- **Communicate:** If texting all day isn't your jam, say so. If it is, make sure the other person is cool with it.

In a world where most messages go something like, "Hey" (five hours later), "Sup," you can be the refreshing exception. With creativity, genuine curiosity, and a dash of effort, your messaging game can turn potential matches into actual connections. So, keep the emojis clever, the banter playful, and don't be afraid to toss out a teasing line now and then. You never know—your next sexy message might just lead to more than a poorly written haiku or a string of heart eyes and fire emojis.

Chapter 7
Zero Dating: The 40-Minute Date Hack You Didn't Know You Needed

Let's talk about *zero dating*—the ultimate dating hack for anyone tired of wasting hours on long, painful first dates that should've ended when they ordered something obnoxious like a triple soy decaf macchiato with extra foam. Shout out to my friend Megan who introduced me to the concept that totally changed my dating life. You know the feeling: you show up full of hope, only to realize within minutes that this person is more like your weird cousin than your future soulmate. Cue the regret as you realize you've just committed to hours of awkward conversation, uncomfortable silences, and some very tense body language.

Enter zero dating, the 40-minute wonder that saves you from all that! Zero dating is the art of quick, no-pressure, casual meet-ups designed to help you feel each other out *without* locking yourself into a marathon of small talk. Think of it as the appetizer to the full-course meal of dating. It's not a commitment; it's a *preview*. You get to see if there's chemistry, intrigue, or just… a mutual sense of "Nah, I'm good," all in under 40 minutes. The best part? You can leave without making excuses or faking a sudden "emergency."

Why Less Is More (Especially in Dating)

Let's be real: the first time you meet someone, it's all about the *vibes*. Are they fun, interesting, and someone you'd want to spend more time with, or are they the human equivalent of lumpy, unseasoned mashed potatoes? Zero dating is the perfect way to find out. By keeping the "date" under 40 minutes, you can avoid the *cringe* of dragging out something that was dead before dessert.

The beauty of zero dating is that it cuts through the nonsense. No need to plan an elaborate dinner or a whole evening around someone you've only exchanged a few texts with. Instead, grab a coffee, take a walk, or meet for a quick drink. Something easy, fun, and non-committal. There's no pressure to impress—just see if you can tolerate being in the same space for over 40 minutes.

The Art of the Zero Date

So, how does one master the zero date? It's simple:

1. **Safety first:** Before heading out on that exciting zero date, let's talk safety. First, always tell a friend where you're going, who you're meeting, and what time you expect to be done. Share your location if you're comfortable—it's better to be over-prepared than under. I also like to share a photo of the person I am going on a date with. It is a fun way to involve your friends by showing them what they look like, and it also helps them know who you are going to see, just in case. I wish this was not the world we lived in, but I have seen too many Dateline episodes not to be prepared. At the end of the day, keeping yourself safe isn't just smart; it's essential. Dating should be fun, but safety always comes first!

2. **Pick a casual location:** A cute coffee shop, a casual bar, or even a walk through the park. Keep it low-key. Bonus points if it's near your escape route (i.e., home or somewhere you can quickly vanish if things get weird).

3. **Set the time frame:** Be upfront—this is a quick meet-up. You're "on your way to something" (even if that something

is Netflix and sweatpants). The key is to give yourself a built-in exit. "I only have about 30–40 minutes, but I'd love to meet up for a quick coffee." See? No pressure.

4. **Keep the conversation light:** This isn't the time to dive into deep conversations about your childhood traumas or the meaning of life. It's about feeling each other out—does their personality match their profile? Are they someone you want to spend more time with?

5. **Gauge the vibe:** By the end of 40 minutes, you should have a solid sense of whether you're into it; if you're vibing, great! You can start planning that *real* first date. If not, you can easily cut things short without the awkward, drawn-out goodbye.

Less Disappointment, More Intrigue

Here's the secret sauce of zero dating: it's low stakes. You're not investing your entire evening (and emotional energy) into someone who could turn out to be a dud. Instead, you're creating space for intrigue. A quick 40-minute meet-up leaves you both wanting more if it goes well. And if it doesn't? No harm, no foul. You walk away with the satisfaction of knowing you didn't just waste your entire night pretending to care about someone's detailed description of their keto diet.

Plus, if the chemistry is there, the zero date leaves you both on a high note—excited for what's to come. You've gotten just enough of a taste to wonder, *"Could there be more?"* And that, my friend, is how you build up to something real. There's no pressure to be perfect or entertain for hours on end; it's just a chance to get acquainted and leave them wanting more.

Sexy, Not Committed

There's something inherently sexy about *not* committing to a long, drawn-out evening. You're mysterious, confident, and in control of your time. Zero dating is for those who know their worth and don't have hours to waste on bad conversation. You get in, feel it out, and either make plans for something more involved or gracefully dip out with your time and dignity intact.

And, let's be inclusive here: zero dating works for *everyone*. Whether you're looking for love, fun, or just seeing who's out there, the zero date keeps things light and easy. It's a quick check to see if the chemistry's right, whether you're looking for a long-term connection or just some flirty banter. No matter who you're into, the zero date is a great way to test the waters without diving into the deep end.

Story Time: The Zero Date Cat-tastrophe

I once had what I thought would be the perfect zero date set up at a local bookstore. A quick, no-pressure meet-up where we could casually browse books, have a light conversation, and keep it under 40 minutes. Easy, right? Famous last words.

I matched with this woman who seemed cool enough in her profile—she was sexy, enjoyed being outdoors, went to loads of concerts, loved books and coffee, and maybe she mentioned her cats, but nothing that raised any red flags. A fellow book lover? Perfect for a bookstore date. Plus, with zero dating, if it didn't work out, I could just get a new title I have been wanting and claim I had "somewhere to be," which, in this case, was literally *anywhere but there*.

We met up at a cozy indie bookstore—one of those places with creaky floors, stacks of books everywhere, and that faint smell of musty paper that makes you feel smarter just for walking in. The first five minutes were fine. We chatted about what we were currently reading, and I made her laugh with some dumb joke about how Jane Austen didn't like to play cards because she didn't like to deal with hearts. She humored me with a sweet giggle and a great smile. But then… it started.

"So, I have three cats," she said, with the intensity of someone about to deliver a TED Talk.

Three? Okay, fine. Cats are not my favorite, but to each their own. I wasn't planning on moving in tomorrow, so I could handle a conversation about three cats.

"They're my babies. I mean, I *talk* to them. They're like, my whole world," she added, moving us from casual cat conversation to what was clearly going to be the full Cat Chronicles. She pulled out her phone to show me a series of photos—cats on the couch, cats on her lap, cats doing… well, cat things. Each one had a *distinct* personality, she assured me.

"Beverly is the moody one, of course. But then there's Myles. He's a total cuddle bug. And Periwinkle? Don't get me started; he's my adventurous one! If you want to follow, I have a whole Instagram dedicated to them."

I was nodding politely, hoping this would naturally run its course—sadly, it did not. We went down the rabbit hole of detailed cat behavior. It was like being held hostage at a feline focus group.

Just when I thought it couldn't get any weirder, she casually dropped, "Oh, and by the way, I know exactly how I'm going to die."

I blinked, caught completely off guard.

"Yeah, I've always had this feeling—this *premonition*—that I'll be hit by a bus," she said, dead serious. "I can just see it happening, you know? I've accepted it."

Okay, *what*?

"So, I don't really worry about anything too much," she continued with an unsettling sense of calm. "I mean, what's the point when you know how it will end, right?"

Now, there's no manual for this kind of conversation. Do you ask follow-up questions? Nod in agreement? Slowly back away? I felt like I'd stumbled into the horror novel section instead of the biography section we were awkwardly browsing. All I could think was: How did we go from these furry felines to impending bus-related doom?

At this point, we were nearing the 30-minute mark, and I had made the executive decision to bail. I glanced at my watch, gave my best "this was fun, but I've gotta run" face, and told her it was nice meeting her, but I had to get going.

She didn't seem phased. In fact, she smiled, patted my arm, and said, "Yeah, I figured. Well, let me know if you ever want to meet the cats! Or, you know, hang out again before the bus thing happens."

As I walked away from the bookstore, I couldn't help but laugh. Zero dating: keeping dates short and saving you from a lifetime of cat photos and existential bus theories.

Story Time Part Deux: The Zero Date That Went from Ice Cream to 40s in the Park

Not all Zero dates end up with you wanting to cough up furballs. When I first met Tristan, I wasn't expecting much—after all, it was a *zero date*. Forty minutes, in and out, no pressure. We'd agreed to meet for ice cream and a walk in the park just to feel things out. Low stakes, no grand expectations. But as soon as we met, something clicked.

We started with ice cream, which, let's be honest, is a solid start to any date. Tristan showed up with this effortlessly cool, laid-back style, and we immediately got into people-watching, cracking jokes about the overly enthusiastic joggers and the guy walking what looked like the world's tiniest dog. The best part about the dog walker was that he looked like a bodybuilder from the 1980s Venice Beach Era in a matching gold tracksuit. We talked about everything and nothing at the same time—our favorite foods, weird childhood stories, and that awkward time when we both went through an ill-advised emo phase. Somehow, we managed to cover both lighthearted banter and deeper conversations in no time.

Suddenly, forty minutes had flown by, and neither of us wanted the conversation to end. So, like the responsible adults we are, we decided the next logical step was to swing by the nearest liquor store, grab a couple of 40s (I was a true Stocktonian and made them into Brass Monkeys, which are Mickeys and Orange Juice, the classiest of all malt liquor cocktails), and continue our chat as we lounged like degenerates in the park.

For the next three hours, we sat on the grass, sipping (okay, chugging) our 40s and talking about everything from our weirdest life experiences to how freeing it was to just be ourselves without expectations.

What was supposed to be a quick, low-stakes zero date turned into this hilarious, carefree hangout session that I still think about. No stress, no "where is this going?"—just two people connecting over ice cream and malt liquor in the park.

Chapter 8
First Date Prep: After the Zero Date, It's Time to Bring Your A-Game

So, you survived the zero date. You navigated the quick coffee meet-up, the casual "get to know you" chat, and somehow, you both left intrigued enough to schedule an *actual* first date. Well done! You've passed the screening round, and now it's time for the main event. No pressure, right?

But here's the thing: first dates are a bit like going on stage—there's a mix of excitement and the underlying hope that you don't completely embarrass yourself. Lucky for you, there's a way to walk into that first date feeling confident, looking great, and ready to bring your A-game. Let's dive in!

1. Wardrobe: The Holy Grail of First Impressions

First things first: what you wear matters. But before you start freaking out and pulling your entire closet onto the bed, let's take a breath. You don't need to look like you're auditioning for a rom-com, but you *do* want to look like you put some effort in. Choose something that makes you feel like a million bucks without looking like you tried too hard. The goal is to strike that balance between "I woke up like this" and "I'm going to the Oscars."

Make sure that you are authentic and genuine. I have talked with so many people who go shopping and spend money on clothes that they don't like and will never wear again. You do not need to do all that. Stick to your style and budget—there's no need to break the bank for a person who might still share a bank account with their ex or sleep in their mom's basement.

Pro Tip: Comfort is key. You won't feel your best if you're tugging at your outfit all night. So, no, this is *not* the time to break in new shoes. Wear something that makes you feel confident but doesn't distract you from having fun.

2. The Pre-Date Pep Talk

Remember: You're a catch. Before leaving the house, give yourself the pep talk you didn't know you needed. Stand in front of the mirror, channel your inner Beyoncé, and remind yourself that you've got this. Talk to yourself the way that you would talk to your best friend unless you have some very toxic, unhealthy relationship there, and do the opposite of that. The zero-date proved you've already piqued their interest, so the hard part is over. Now, it's just about being your fabulous, perfectly imperfect self.

Pro Tip: If you need a little extra boost, play your go-to hype song while you're getting ready. Whether it's Lizzo, AC/DC, Ruby Waters (If you don't know her, you should. She is a goddamn goddess), or whatever gets you feeling like a rockstar, let the music put you in the right mood.

3. Nope, Not Today: The Art of First-Date Boundaries

Setting boundaries on a first date is like being the bouncer for your own personal comfort zone—you decide what stays and what goes, no velvet ropes required. It's about keeping things fun and cozy without wandering into territory that will have you looking at the nearest exit. Whether it's drawing the line at sharing too much ex-drama or making it clear that you're good with a handshake (and *not* a spontaneous hand-holding marathon with Clammy Hands McGee), boundaries are the magic ingredient for a relaxed, low-stress vibe.

Do you have a two-drink limit because you don't want to turn into the "Did I already tell you this story?" person? Say it. Are you not keen on discussing your five-year plan within the first 20 minutes? That's fine too—remember, it's a date, not a therapy session. Boundaries are your best friend if you're already feeling overwhelmed before the appetizer hits. And yes, they can keep things playful and spontaneous without leaving you wondering how to navigate "Is it cool if we order for each other?" territory.

And if things start getting weird (like "Let's split dessert even though I haven't touched my entrée" weird), boundaries give you the perfect exit strategy. They're there to ensure you're having a good time without feeling like you must start mapping out a plan B. Here's the truth: Anyone worth a second date will appreciate that you know what works for you and are happy to play by your rules.

---

4. Conversation Game: Keep It Fun, Keep It Real

This isn't a police interrogation. You're not there to grill each other on life goals, debt, and childhood traumas (save that for date #5). Instead, consider this a chance to get to know each other better in a relaxed setting. You already know you're interested, so let the conversation flow naturally.

Keep it witty; keep it light. Throw in a few playful comments, ask questions, and—most importantly—listen. There's nothing worse than someone who monopolizes the conversation without letting the other person get a word in. Remember, you're looking for a spark, not trying to solve the world's problems over spring rolls.

Pro Tip: Avoid diving too deep into ex-talk, politics, or anything that could kill the vibe. If things start heading toward "So, my ex once…" territory, hit the eject button and steer the conversation toward something more fun—like dream vacations, favorite types of music, or books they have read recently.

---

5. *Smell Good, but Don't Overdo It*

We've all been there—someone walks into the room, and it smells like they've been baptized in the entire cologne section of a department store. You want to smell good, not take someone to their knees with a single whiff. A light spritz of your favorite scent is perfect—enough to make a statement without causing a sensory overload.

Remember, subtlety is key. Your scent should be a pleasant surprise, not an all-encompassing cloud that announces your arrival five minutes before you walk in. Think of your fragrance like a whisper, not a shout. You want your date to lean in because they're intrigued, not trying to identify that overpowering aroma.

Also, take the setting and the time of day into account. A heavy, musky scent might be great for an evening out, but for a daytime coffee date? Not so much. Opt for lighter, fresher scents during the day and save those deeper fragrances for nighttime rendezvous. Matching your scent to the occasion shows thoughtfulness—and that you have a handle on basic social cues, which is always a plus.

And please, for the love of all things nasal, avoid the temptation to layer multiple scented products. If your soap, shampoo, deodorant, aftershave, and cologne have different fragrances, you're creating a symphony that no one wants to hear—or smell. Stick to one or two complementary scents to keep things harmonious. Your goal is to smell good, not to smell like the entire perfume counter at Macy's.

Let's not forget about personal space. Strong scents can be invasive; some people are sensitive or even allergic. You don't want your date's eyes watering because your perfume is staging a full-frontal assault on their senses. Nothing kills the mood faster than a sneezing fit or a sudden asthma attack.

Finally, if you're unsure about how much is too much, err on the side of caution. You can always do a quick refresh in the restroom if needed, but it's much harder to dial it back once you've gone overboard. Remember, your scent should invite someone closer, not force them to maintain a safe distance.

So, spritz wisely, my friend. A little mystery goes a long way, and less is definitely more when it comes to fragrance. After all, you want them to remember *you*, not just the cloud of eau de toilette you left behind.

6. Plan Something Casual but Fun

This isn't the time to plan a three-course dinner with wine pairings or make dinner reservations at a place where the tablecloths cost more than your grocery bill. Keep it casual, keep it light, and keep it fun. A cozy bar, a laid-back restaurant, or something interactive—think mini-golf, bowling, or a trivia night—gives you something to do besides trying to fill awkward silences over an oversized plate of pasta. The goal here isn't to impress/possibly intimidate them with culinary expertise or wine knowledge; it's to have a good time, get a feel for each other's vibe, and, ideally, laugh a little.

Interactive dates are a total win because they take the pressure off forced conversation. Having something to do can be a lifesaver for those inevitable pauses that pop up as you get to know each other. Nothing fills a silence quite like a playful putt-putt challenge or rallying as a team to answer random trivia questions. Plus, it allows you to show off your competitive or collaborative side in a way that "Would you like some more bread?" just doesn't quite capture.

Pro Tip: Add a second location or a little adventure (even something as simple as walking to grab dessert afterward). This naturally extends the date, takes the edge off, and adds variety—making it feel like you're exploring together, not just sitting through a restaurant ritual. It also gives you a built-in transition if things are going well or a natural exit if they're not. Suppose things are clicking; great! Keep it going. If not? "Thanks for the game, let's split that check" has never been easier.

The best first dates are simple, low-pressure, and have a touch of spontaneity—after all, you're testing chemistry here, not auditioning for Top Chef. So, pick something easy, keep the vibe light, and remember that a casual, fun date leaves room for genuine connection without the pretense.

---

7. *Manage Your Expectations (Because This Is Real Life)*

Sure, we've all seen those movie-worthy first dates where everything flows, sparks fly, the lighting is perfect, *and* a double rainbow is seen in the sky. The conversation is witty, there's magical chemistry, and nobody even *thinks* about spilling their drink. I hate to break it to you, dear reader, but real life? It's usually more like an outtake reel. Your date might trip over their words, you could knock over a glass of water, and the restaurant might be fresh out of your favorite dish. Heck, maybe you'll end up at a table with a wobbly leg, dodging the weird draft from the AC vent above. *It happens.* Take a breath.

Expecting a fairy-tale evening is a lot of pressure to put on yourself and the poor person sitting across from you, who's probably just as nervous. Instead of aiming for a rom-com movie, focus on enjoying *this* moment, with all its quirks and imperfections. Maybe your date is trying to impress you with their sushi knowledge and mispronounces "sashimi," or perhaps you both realize halfway through that neither of you even like the restaurant you picked. It's okay. Take each funny mishap as part of the charm—these small, unexpected moments make for the best memories (and stories to tell later).

Pro Tip: Sometimes, the best dates are the imperfect ones. They're the ones where you're laughing over how ridiculous things got or realizing that you can both laugh off awkward moments. Embrace the spills, the wobbly table, the overenthusiastic waiter, the slightly awkward goodbyes. This is real life, and these little moments make dating memorable.

---

8. Don't Forget to Be Yourself (Yes, Really)

This is the golden rule of dating—or life in general, really. There's absolutely no point in pretending to be someone you're not. Unless you're a secret agent on an undercover mission (in which case, you've got bigger things to worry about), embracing who you are is the way to go. If you're sarcastic, let that sarcasm shine, baby. If you're a bit quirky, whether that means you collect vintage lunchboxes or have an encyclopedic knowledge of obscure '80s cartoons, own it!

Authenticity is way sexier than molding yourself into what you think they want. Remember, you've already made it to the first date—something about the real you caught their attention. Now's the time to show them more of that, not less. Trying to be someone else is not only exhausting but also unsustainable. Eventually, the facade will slip, possibly at an awkward moment, like when you accidentally geek out over the comic bookstore you pass by.

Being yourself sets the tone for the entire relationship. Do you want to start things off with an Oscar-worthy performance of "Ideal Date Version of Me," and six months later, you completely meltdown because you can't stand the beach and yet agree to a week-long trip to the Bahamas? Didn't think so. Plus, embracing your true self encourages your date to relax and be more authentic. It's a win-win where everyone gets to be real, and who knows—you might discover shared interests you wouldn't have found otherwise.

Pro Tip: Confidence comes from owning your quirks, not hiding them. People are naturally drawn to those comfortable in their skin—it's magnetic. Be unapologetically yourself because that's the person they're here to get to know. If you love pun-filled jokes, drop one into the conversation. If you're passionate about environmental causes, talk about it. Your enthusiasm can be infectious.

And here's the kicker: if they don't appreciate the real you, it's better to find out sooner rather than later. Authenticity acts as a filter, weeding out those who aren't a good fit and saving you time and energy in the long run. Remember, the goal isn't just to impress someone on a first date; it's to connect with someone who appreciates you for you.

So go ahead and let your freak flag fly (within reason). Wear that bold outfit that makes you feel fabulous, share your honest opinions, and laugh loudly if something tickles you. After all, life is too short to play a watered-down version of yourself, and dating is too challenging to add an extra layer of pretense and complication. Embrace the awkward, the unique, the genuine—you might just find that's exactly what they've been looking for.

---

9. The "Just in Case" Exit Strategy

Even if things are going great, having an exit plan is always good—just in case. Sometimes, despite the best intentions and a great profile, the connection isn't there. Maybe they're sneakily looking at profiles on Bumble under the table and forget that there is a mirror behind them (True Story!), or they have a personality that doesn't quite match their witty messages. Or perhaps you're just not feeling that elusive *spark*. Whatever the reason, having a pre-planned, graceful way to cut the date short is always a smart move.

It doesn't have to be dramatic or hurtful—in fact, it's best to keep things polite and positive. A quick, "Hey, I've got to get up early tomorrow, but this was fun!" or "I have plans after this, but let's catch up soon" works wonders for a smooth exit. It's light and respectful, allowing you to leave with your head high. This way, you're sparing yourself and your date the uncomfortable dance of lingering when things aren't clicking.

And let's talk about *how* to exit—because a good exit strategy means keeping it simple. Excuses about fictional sick friends, dramatic "emergencies," or fake work emails just aren't necessary. A polite "Thank you for the evening" shows respect and avoids unnecessary complications or awkwardness. Plus, you'll feel better about your honesty and won't have to worry about running into them again with a tale you can't back up.

Pro Tip: No need to ghost anyone. If it's not a match, be direct but kind. After the date, a simple message like, "I didn't feel a connection, but I had a good time" is all it takes to close the door gracefully. Not every date will lead to fireworks, and that's okay! Part of dating is realizing that sometimes there's no chemistry and nothing wrong with acknowledging it gently and moving on.

---

10. Post-Date Debrief (with Snacks)

After the date, it's time to unwind and reflect. Grab your favorite snack, your beverage of choice, kick off your shoes, and take a few moments to ask yourself some honest questions. How did it go? Did you enjoy yourself? Did they make you laugh, or did you mentally scroll through your to-do list for the rest of the week? Did the conversation flow, or were you grasping for topics because you felt you had to? Reflect on the chemistry—or lack—and trust your gut. Sometimes, you just *know* when there's something worth exploring further; other times, you can feel that it's better left as a one-time thing.

If you're genuinely excited to see them again, fantastic! But if you're on the fence, don't force it. The beauty of first dates is that they're just the beginning—if it's a fit, you'll know; if not, there's always someone else out there. And don't underestimate the power of your intuition; those little hunches often tell you a lot about whether you're intrigued or just being polite.

Pro Tip: Text a friend and give them the full rundown—because the post-date debrief is almost as important as the date itself. Your friends are probably waiting for the details anyway, and it helps to get another perspective. Plus, they know you well and can often help you see things more clearly. Did you light up while discussing the date, or did you spend more time discussing the snack you're eating now? Sometimes, the way you recount the date reveals more than you think.

At the end of the day, it's about trusting yourself and letting things unfold naturally. First dates are a chance to see if there's something worth building on, not an audition for the role of a lifetime. So relax, embrace the experience, and remember: there's no need to rush or settle—just enjoy the ride.

Rocci's Controversial Thoughts About Who Picks Up the Check:

Let's talk about paying for first dates—a topic as divisive as political discussions at the dinner table. My rule? We split it right down the middle. I know, for some, that's a scandalous stance. But hear me out: if the goal of a first date is to get to know each other, I don't see why one person should be footing the bill like they're trying to woo a 19th-century duchess from Bridgerton.

To me, halving the first date sets the tone for partnership, not patronage. You're both here as two grown adults (hopefully) scoping out the situation, so why put the financial burden on one person? Here's my go-to: we split the first, they can grab the second, and I'll cover the third. After that, it's a free-for-all of

Venmo charges, round-buying, and spontaneous generosity—*because that's equality, baby.*

Think of it this way: you're setting the stage for a balanced, equal playing field where no one feels obligated or like they've signed a low-key rental agreement for the evening. Besides, if we're chipping in, we have a little skin in the game. It's a signal that we're in this together—not that one of us is out here hosting the other like a charity auction. So go ahead and order those fancy cocktails because we're both taking ownership of this date—and that's how you know it's real.

Story Time: The Date Where Everything Went Wrong (But Somehow Still Went Right)

Sometimes, you have to just trust the process because, on paper, the date could be horrible but turn out amazing. Let me set the scene: it was supposed to be a regular first date at this cozy little restaurant. You know, the kind of place with mood lighting, jazz music, and a specialty cocktail list that screams, "I'm sophisticated, and I am going to pay 20 dollars to show you". I was excited, but also keeping my expectations in check. I didn't expect the evening to turn into an episode of *Kitchen Nightmares* meets *Bar Rescue*—starring us.

It all started innocently enough. My date—let's call him Grant—was charming, confident, and had this infectious humor. He was handsome and smart and had traveled the world, which we could talk about forever since I also love to travel. However, I am a cheap traveler, so check out my fourth book, "Passport, Pennies, and Pleasantries: A Broke Traveler's Guide to Annoying Locals (But in a Fun Way)."

Back to the story… The conversation flowed, the banter was quick, and I was having fun. Things were going suspiciously well… almost *too* well.

Now, Grant seemed like the kind of guy who knew his way around a menu, but when dessert time rolled around, he decided to up the ante. We ordered Bananas Foster (because why not go for the flaming dessert on a first date, right?). But when the waiter showed up and started preparing it tableside, Grant decided to intervene in all his suave, confident glory.

"Hey man, would you mind if I showed off a little to this beautiful woman and did the dessert for us? I used to work in a restaurant and did hundreds of these a week." Grant said, in what can only be described as a serious case of overconfidence. The waiter, bless his soul, looked around for someone to save him, and Grant gave him his most sincere smile and said, "Trust me." I just stood there as Grant took over, clearly determined to show off his supposed flaming dessert skills.

As Grant tried to perform what I can only assume was his attempt at a culinary flourish, things quickly spiraled out of control. He added a little too much rum to the mix, and before anyone could react, *whoosh*—the flames jumped a little higher than expected. And then, like a scene from a movie, Grant's hair—yes, his hair— caught fire.

I froze, not entirely sure if I was on a date or somehow traveled back in time to Micheal Jackson's Pepsi Commercial (For my younger generations, please google. This joke only works if you understand the context. Totally worth it, right? Thank you for humoring me). But Grant? The man stayed calm—cooler than anyone with flaming hair should ever be. He quickly patted his head, extinguished the flames, and laughed it off like this was just a regular Tuesday night. The smell of burnt hair and embarrassment filled the room as the poor waiter looked around as if he was about to be fired. Grant quickly took his seat and said, "On second thought, why don't you take over." This now terrified young man went behind the portable stove and did a great job not setting his face on fire. We enjoyed our dessert, which had the pungent aroma of burnt hair and shame.

Now, this could have been a disastrous end to our date, but Grant did a great job owning up to being a little cocky with his skill sets and was checking in with me to make sure I wasn't ashamed to be seen with him. Little does he know I do not feel shame... even when I should. He asked if I wanted to go somewhere for a nightcap, and I agreed, so we made our way to a quaint little wine bar around the corner, and the night just continued to get more interesting.

Here's a fun fact about me: I wear many hats in all aspects of my life, including my work life. I work in mental health, I own my own criminal justice reform consulting business, I do data analysis and grant writing for state and local agencies, I am now a ***distinguished*** author (too soon?), and I bartend for fun. I know you may be thinking that I have some sort of personality disorder, and the jury is still out on that one and will inform the title of my 5th book, "Six Jobs, Zero Chill: Confessions of a Woman Who Can't Stop Hustling."

Anyways, this wine bar is adorable. It has great mood lighting, sexy music playing, beautiful people to look at, and what looks like a bartender who has been on a three-day bender. The bartender—who had clearly been sampling too much of their product—was stumbling around behind the bar, incapable of pouring anything more complicated than water. They were bleary-eyed, asking guests to repeat things, pouring white wines instead of red, and counting out change incorrectly. The last straw for them was when they dropped a whole bottle of Champagne, and it broke into a million pieces on the ground. After that graceful act, they said, and I quote, "Fuck this, I need a cigarette," and they walked out the front door. This left Grant, me, and about ten other people looking around wide-eyed at each other.

Another fun fact about me, I have worked in the service industry for over 15 years, so if I am at a restaurant or a bar and they are struggling, you better believe that my ass is going to help out. To all my service industry people out there thank you for what you do. You do not hear that enough, and you deal with so much bullshit it is not even funny. I think every person in the world should have to work for one year in retail or the service industry and one year in education before they are allowed to have a career job. If everyone did that, I believe we would have fewer Kyles out there and a lot more patient, kind Karens. Again, you are welcome, Karens.

Anyways... Cue me, stepping up to the plate.

"I've got this," I said to Grant as I took the wine key out of my purse. Yes, I carry a wine key. My older sister, Nicole, who better be reading this, always taught me to be prepared, including having at least one wine key on your person at all times.

This was a wine bar primarily, but it did have a full bar as well, and thank god for that because my knowledge of wine ends at screw top or cork. Everyone looks at me a little crazy at first, but I go to the first person and say, "What will it be?" they reluctantly say, "Tom Collins and a Pinot Noir for her." I asked him if he used to drink those in the war because only hundred-year-old men drink Tom Collins, and he laughed, and everyone relaxed a little.

Luckily, this place's operating system is one that I use at my bar, so it was easy to navigate. The guy pays for the drinks, tips me 20%, and goes to sit down. The next one in line is Grant. He looks at me and says, "Was this all a part of your plan to get into my pants? Because I have to tell you, it is working." I reminded him that if I really wanted to be in his pants, I wouldn't have bothered with a nightcap and let him know he was holding up the line. He ordered sex on the beach just to be annoying, and I knew that I was going to like this guy. I make the drink for him and end up working at the bar for over an hour before the manager walks in. He takes one look at me and says, "Who the hell are you?" I looked back and could not resist saying, "Captain. Captain Save a Hoe, Sir. At your service." Grant spit out his sex on the beach, but the manager looked less than amused. I explained the situation and he went in the back to watch the security tapes to confirm my story and then offered me a job on the spot now that he had an opening. I thanked him but shared that I already had too many jobs and was on a first date. He took care of our tab, and we got ready to go.

By the end of the night, we had managed to survive flaming desserts, impromptu bartending, and one very wasted mixologist. But more importantly, we had a blast. We got to know each other through all the chaos, and instead of the date falling apart, it felt like we were in on this hilarious, absurd adventure together.

Who knew that watching your date literally set his hair on fire could be the spark that led to a story-worthy first date?

Chapter 9

The Truth Bomb: Why You Should Share Your Secrets Before Things Get Weird

Alright, I may be saying something controversial, and many of you may want to close the book now and decide to leave me a nasty review on Goodreads (Also, I have decided that I will only read my bad reviews in a Mickey Mouse voice so the joke is on you, that is going to be hilarious no matter what you write). I will stick by what I am about to say. YOU SHOULD BE HONEST ABOUT POTENTIAL DEAL BREAKERS ON DATES! First dates are basically like job interviews for your love life. Sure, you're testing the waters, but this isn't just about how cute you look sipping that cocktail. It's about making sure you're not wasting your time on someone who has a bombshell waiting to drop, like, "Oh, by the way, I'm still married. But don't worry, we're *separated*... we just live together for now."

So, what *should* you disclose early on? You don't need to bare your soul or list your deepest insecurities, but certain details are non-negotiable. Think of it as giving your date the courtesy of an informed decision before they fall headfirst for your charming smile and sharp wit. This does not necessarily need to be on the first date, but my rule is that it needs to be before date three or, for sure, before anything gets intimate. If you enjoy being intimate early on, you must be prepared to share these things quickly. Let's go through some common things that could be early deal breakers for some.

1. Are You Married (Or Still Technically Married)?

Yeah, this one's a biggie. If you're still technically someone's spouse, your date might want to know that *before* they start planning date two. Sure, separation is messy, but honesty? That's just polite.

What to Say: "So, I'm going through a separation right now. It is a process we want to be intentional about, but I figured I should put that out there and make sure to answer any questions you may have.

---

2. Do You Have Kids?

Many people have this information on their profiles, but some want to be a little more discreet regarding their family lives. Whether you've got one toddler or a whole soccer team at home, this is information that your date might want upfront. It's not a dealbreaker for everyone, but it's definitely not something you want to casually slip in on date three, like, "Oh, did I mention I have twins?"

What to Say: "By the way, I've got two amazing kids who're a huge part of my life. Just thought I'd share that in case it's important to you."

---

3. Are You Looking to Get Married?

Some people are swiping for a spouse; others are swiping for something less permanent. If you're dating with the long game in mind—or absolutely *not*—it's good to let that slip early on. It doesn't need to be a proposal, but knowing where each of you stands saves a lot of awkward "what are we?" conversations.

What to Say: "I'm not saying I'm picking out wedding venues, but I'm definitely dating to find something serious. How about you?"

---

4. Quirks, Oddities, and Fun Facts

Do you only have three toes? Maybe you have a pet tarantula you *insist* on having on your shoulder while you watch *Love Island*. These might not seem like date-one topics, but hey, it's better to find out now than when you're three months in, and they scream at the sight of your furry-legged roommate.

What to Say: "This might be a little weird, but I've got a pet tarantula named Fluffy. He's a sweetie, but I figured I should mention it upfront."

---

5. Financial or Career Goals (or Lack Thereof)

You don't need to whip out your Excel Spreadsheet or your entire financial portfolio, but if your life plan involves quitting your job to become a full-time influencer or moving to a remote island to write poetry, that might be worth mentioning. Some people are into it; some people aren't. Transparency is key.

What to Say: "I'm planning to take a year off work to travel and start a YouTube channel. Is that something you're cool with?"

6. Dealbreakers You Can't Ignore

If you're someone who's 100% sure about wanting kids—or 100% sure you *don't*—it's a good idea to bring that up sooner rather than later. Some people cannot stand smokers; others need a partner who enjoys staying in at least 4 nights a week. It is okay to have dealbreakers as long as they are reasonable and not ten pages long. Nobody wants to be three dates in and suddenly realize they're on completely different life paths.

What to Say: "Just so we're on the same page, I'm not looking to have kids in the future. I hope that's cool with you."

Story Time: Girl With A Van Down By The River

It started off like the kind of love story that would give a rom-com screenwriter a full-on boner: two free-spirited souls meet, bond over their love for hole-in-the-wall eateries, debate over the best novels of the year, and spend entire evenings roasting hipster craft beers. She was bright, sexy, and had apparently seen more countries than I'd seen Keanu Reeves films (Which is all of them, btw that is 73 films for anyone who would like that nugget of information for their next trivia night). Her bohemian vibe? On point. She insisted cars were environmental atrocities on par with using baby seals as ottomans—so I figured she was one of those eco-warrior types who lounged in a Pinterest-perfect tiny house near some solar-powered coffee shop.

For two months, everything was great. Well, almost everything. Every time the night wound down, I'd suggest going to her place for a change. You know—so I wouldn't have to keep hosting her, and my fridge wouldn't continue to suffer catastrophic wine and cheese shortages. But she'd always shrug me off, saying something like, "I prefer the lighting at your place" or "My place is too far." She even made me feel guilty for driving my car since she biked everywhere. And I let her because I was under the impression she was out there saving baby whales between yoga classes.

Then came the night that changed it all. She had a few too many drinks, and we got into a fight—she accused me of batting my eyelashes at some random woman (I don't think I have the demeanor for eyelash-batting, but okay). She got loud, she got feisty, and she demanded I take her home immediately. I admitted I had zero clue where she lived, so she grabbed my phone and dropped a pin. Then, as if on cue, she passed out, leaving me navigating the GPS to what I assumed was her minimalist eco-chateau or perhaps a yurt surrounded by organic kale fields.

Fifteen minutes later, I was driving under an overpass that looked like Mad Max was hosting a yard sale. Rows of sketchy vans, half-dead RVs, and maybe a cardboard castle or two. I woke her up, gently nudged her shoulder, and said, "Uh, I think you put the pin in the wrong place—I'm pretty sure we took a wrong turn into a zombie apocalypse."

She opened one eye, pointed at a dented van that had definitely seen more oil changes than interior cleanings, and slurred, "That's my place, dummy." I must have stared at her as she'd just recited the entire Tibetan Book of the Dead in Klingon because she immediately got defensive: "Don't you judge me! It's not my fault I got that third DUI and lost my car, house, and job! I was barely over the legal limit!"

And just like that, the bohemian mystique popped like a cheap balloon. Suddenly, her "flexible schedule" sounded less like freelance artistry and more like "unemployed and sleeping in a van." Her disdain for cars wasn't a moral stance but a practical necessity since, you know, no license. That international traveler persona might have been more about skipping town and avoiding court dates than hopping countries.

I'm not saying I'm perfect—I've got skeletons, sure, but they're more of the "I sometimes get kicked out of bars in Mexico/Ireland/Greece" variety. This was a whole different level. Turns out, the only world-changing she was doing involved dodging cops and parking tickets under a bridge.

So yeah, that was our last romantic evening. I left her in that broken-down van, feeling like I'd just been punked by the universe. Let's just say next time someone guilt-trips me about my car's carbon footprint, I'm going to politely ask to see their license.

The Bottom Line: Honesty Saves Everyone's Time

Look, dating is complicated enough without holding back the stuff that matters. Being upfront with your date about the big things—marital status, kids, housing situation, future goals, and yes, even weird quirks—helps keep things real. And trust me, it's way better to find out early on if you're compatible rather than six months down the line when someone's sharing that they cannot have Fluffy near them while watching TV. Honesty doesn't just make things easier it also makes things more fun when your "big reveal" is more of a shared laugh than a dealbreaker. You may also find some common ground or even common quirks you were not expecting.

Chapter 10
Ghosting: The Ultimate Vanishing Act

Ghosting—it's the ultimate disappearing act, like dating's version of Houdini, but with none of the magic tricks and all the *Abracadabras*. One minute, you're chatting, maybe even making plans for the weekend, and the next, *poof*—they're gone. No goodbye, no explanation, just a sudden, eerie silence that makes you wonder if they joined a secret government agency overnight.

Let's be honest: ghosting is the ultimate dating cop-out. Why have an awkward conversation when you can disappear into the abyss like a ninja with commitment issues? It's the adult equivalent of ducking behind the couch when the doorbell rings and pretending you're not home—except instead of a delivery person, it's someone who thought you were interested in them.

The Classic Ghosting Scenario

It starts like any other conversation. You're hitting it off, sharing memes, maybe even chatting about dream vacation spots, and you start thinking, "Okay, this could go somewhere!" Then, like clockwork, their responses get a little... slower. First, it takes an hour for them to respond, then two hours, and eventually, you're staring at your phone, waiting for that "Hey, sorry, I was busy" message that *never* comes.

You check their profile to make sure they didn't block you (don't lie, we've all done it), and you notice they're still posting stories on Instagram. So, they're alive—just not alive for *you*. And that's when it hits you: you've been ghosted.

The "Did I Say Something?" Spiral

After the initial shock of ghosting wears off, you enter the "Did I Say Something Wrong?" phase. You start replaying every message you sent. Was it that joke that people who like pineapple on pizza are scientifically all serial killers? Or maybe they didn't like that I used too many emojis in response to their last message. Was my last "LOL" too aggressive? It's a spiral that can drive anyone to the brink of texting a desperate, "Hey, did I do something?" message, which—let me tell you—is a guaranteed way to never hear from them again.

Ghosting makes even the most confident dater feel like they've just bombed a stand-up comedy set. One minute, you're riding high; the next, you're questioning whether you've accidentally become the dating world's worst conversationalist.

The "Ghoster" Archetypes

Some of my friends have not even realized that they have been ghosted, so why don't we venture through the graveyard and check out the different ghosts that are out there (Cue spooky music):

1. **The Silent Phantom:** This is the most classic ghost. They disappear without a word, leaving you to wonder if they were just a figment of your imagination. They don't block you—they just slip away, probably thinking they're sparing you from an awkward conversation when, in reality, they're just being rude.

2. **The Semi-Ghost:** This ghost doesn't completely vanish—they just start to fade into the background, like an extra in a movie who is technically still there but doesn't really matter. They'll reply to your messages once every few days, just enough to keep you on the hook but never enough

to actually make plans. Their texts get shorter. They stop initiating conversations. "Hey, how's it going?" turns into a single "K" reply, and you're left wondering where all those letters and that witty banter went. They'll still respond to you, just enough to keep the hope alive. But it's like trying to hold onto smoke. You want to believe they're just "busy," but deep down, you know they're slowly fading into the background, about to pull a full ghost at any moment. It's like watching someone back out of a room really slowly, pretending they're still interested until they're just a speck on the horizon.

3. **The "Ghosted After the Date":** This one's a real gut punch. You've gone on a great first date—or so you thought. You laughed, you connected, maybe even flirted a bit. The vibe was *there*. Maybe there was a goodnight kiss or at least the promise of seeing each other again. You part ways, thinking, "Wow, that went really well." You send a follow-up text the next day, something breezy like, "Had a great time! Let's do it again soon." And then… nothing. Crickets. Days pass. No response. You've officially been ghosted *after* what felt like a successful date. Now, you're left wondering if you imagined the whole thing. Did they not enjoy the date as much as you thought? Did they hate the fact that you ordered a salad *and* fries? Were they secretly tracking how often you glanced at your phone during dinner? The possibilities are endless, and none of them are good. You spend the next week replaying every second of the date in your head, trying to pinpoint where things went wrong.

4. **The Ghoster Who Goes Out with a Bang:** Some ghosts don't just fade into the night—they go out with a full,

dramatic exit. It's like they're starring in a soap opera and want their grand finale. One moment, things are fine. You're talking, maybe even planning the next date. Then they hit you with a bombshell text like, "I need to focus on myself right now" or "I've decided to move to Bali and find inner peace." These ghosters give you a parting gift in the form of a vague, overly dramatic excuse just before they disappear forever. The message usually leaves you more confused than if they'd just vanished without a word. Are they really moving to Bali? Or is that just code for, "I've already matched with five other people, and you're no longer a priority?"

5. **The Serial Ghoster:** This one's truly baffling because it's not the first time they've ghosted you. Oh no, this is their *thing*. You match with them, talk for a while, and things seem promising. Then they ghost. Weeks (or even months) later, they slide back into your messages like nothing happened: "Hey, it's been a while; how have you been?" You'll think, "Okay, maybe they had something going on; let's give it another try." So, you start talking again. Things pick up where they left off. You even go on a date or two, and then—boom—they ghost you *again*. At this point, you're not even surprised. It's like their dating M.O.: pop in, disappear, come back, repeat. Are they just waiting until they're bored with everyone else before coming back around to you? Are you their emotional support person they ghost when they feel overwhelmed? Whatever it is, it's *exhausting*, and we are no one's sloppy seconds. #noonessloppyseconds.

6. **The Social Media Ghost:** Ghosting can happen in the world of dating apps, but it can also spill over into social

media territory, adding an extra layer of awkwardness. You've been talking, maybe went on a few dates, and then... radio silence. But here's the twist—they don't unfriend you on Instagram. No, they still like your photos, watch your stories, and maybe even occasionally comment on your posts with a little thumbs-up emoji. It's like they want to ghost you but also remind you that they're still around. They're lurking in the background like a digital ghost, still part of your social media life but refusing to engage meaningfully. They'll ghost you in text, but they can't seem to fully let go of the idea of keeping tabs on you. It's like they want to keep a toe in the water, just in case they want to swim back into your life.

Ghosting is the Ultimate Lazy Move

Let's call ghosting what it is: the laziest move in the dating playbook. A simple "I'm not feeling it" or "Hey, I don't think this is going to work" takes, what, 10 seconds to type? Instead, the ghoster opts for the awkward long game of avoidance. They don't realize that ghosting *creates* more awkwardness, not less. Because guess what? Now, when we run into each other in public, it will be all kinds of uncomfortable. And I will *definitely* make a point of saying, "Hey! I am so glad to see you are still alive. I assumed that you died because I would never have thought you would be the coward who couldn't just tell a girl you weren't feeling it" in the most public place possible. Again, I should have shame, but I really don't, so the joke is on you ghoster.

Story Time: The Disappearing Act

Let me tell you about the time I got ghosted by someone who was practically planning our wedding one day and then vanished the next. We had been talking for a few weeks, and things were going great—there was flirting, inside jokes, and even talks of going on a weekend trip together. Yes, a weekend trip! This person was making *plans*.

And then... nothing. No explanation, no goodbye—just radio silence. Naturally, I went through the five stages of ghosting grief: confusion, overthinking, anger, acceptance, and, finally, eating an entire pizza while watching *The Office*.

Two weeks later, they reappeared with the classic line, "Sorry I've been MIA, things got crazy." Crazy? CRAZY? Honey, I've been mentally rewriting your obituary, thinking you got taken by the mob or aliens. Your obituary would read as follows:

Obituary for the Mysteriously Departed: Alexis "The Vanisher" Smith

It is with a mix of bemusement and a hint of sarcasm that we announce the sudden disappearance of Alexis "The Vanisher" Smith, who ghosted us all at the tender age of "it's complicated."

Alexis burst into our lives like a comet—bright, enthusiastic, and impossible to ignore. For a brief period, they dazzled us with grand plans for future adventures, spontaneous getaways, and a happily ever after that sounded almost too good to be true.

Last seen juggling over-the-top romantic gestures and cryptic text messages, Alexis vanished without a trace. Some say a secretive mob family recruited them after displaying an uncanny ability to disappear; others believe he was abducted by aliens seeking expert advice on mixed signals and the art of ghosting. The sudden absence has left a void roughly the size of their unfulfilled promises.

In honor of Alexis's enigmatic life, a memorial service will not be held—mostly because we can't seem to find them. Instead, we encourage friends and acquaintances to commemorate their memory by leaving on read receipts and practicing the fine art of not taking ourselves too seriously.

Alexis is survived by a collection of unread messages, a playlist of love songs that now feels a tad overzealous, and a group of mildly perplexed individuals who wonder if they just dated a figment of their imagination.

In lieu of flowers, please send UFO sighting reports or any information leading to a possible mob connection to your local FBI office. While their physical presence was fleeting, the comedic value of their exit is eternal.

Rest in peace, Alexis—wherever you are, we hope there's decent Wi-Fi.

It turns out that "crazy" just meant that you were seeing someone else and either got bored or it didn't work out and wanted to see if I was still available to give them attention. Spoiler alert: I was not.

Ghosting is really where the art of avoidance meets peak dating frustration! Ghosting stories can range from mildly annoying to downright bewildering. The experience itself is so varied that every dater has their version of the infamous vanishing act.

So, Why Do People Ghost?

The reasons for ghosting are as varied as the people who do it. Some ghost because they're conflict-avoidant, others because they're just not that interested, and a few might be serial ghosters who do it because they like to keep things casual and also do not like to be alone. And then there are those who ghost because they're juggling too many matches and don't know how to prioritize their time without dropping someone (which, honestly, is still rude).

But the real reason ghosting happens? It's the easy way out. No one wants to have that "I'm not interested" conversation, so they disappear instead. Ghosting is the ultimate shortcut for people who don't want to deal with the awkwardness. It's not great, but it's become the norm in the age of dating apps and instant communication.

The Bottom Line on Ghosting

Ghosting is frustrating, confusing, and downright rude, but it's also one of those inevitable experiences in the world of online dating. The good news? Ghosting teaches you to value clear communication and respect in future connections. And it helps you spot the red flags sooner. After all, do you really want to date someone who can't even muster the courage to say, "Hey, I don't think this is working out."

Ghosting may be frustrating, but it's also the universe's way of clearing out the dead weight. The people who stick around? Those are the ones worth your time. And while ghosting is annoying and confusing, just remember: you're the one who dodged the awkwardness. They're the ones who'll have to explain why they disappeared when they inevitably run into you at the grocery store, and you hand them that obituary you wrote for them. Awkward for them, empowering for you.

At the end of the day, ghosting isn't about you—it's about the ghoster's inability to communicate and is a sign of their lack of overall maturity. So, if you've been ghosted, don't take it personally. Move on, keep swiping, and save your energy for someone who's actually going to stick around.

Chapter 11

The Break-It-Gently Handbook: How to Say "Thanks, but No Thanks" After a Few Dates

So, you've gone on a few dates, shared some laughs, maybe even swapped quirky stories about your childhood pets or how you didn't get picked for the dodgeball team that one time, but now… it's just *not* clicking. Whether it's the chemistry, the conversation, or their tendency to overshare about their "creative" sock collection, you've realized this isn't going anywhere.

Here's the thing: telling someone you're not interested doesn't have to feel like pulling teeth out of the mouth of a radioactive shark. It's all about being honest, kind, and—most importantly—empowered. We want to respect everyone's time, energy, and feelings, so if you are not into it, you must be honest about it. We have all been on the receiving end of the cliché "It's not you, it's me" or "I'm not really looking for a relationship right now." Or my personal favorite, "I need to work on myself." It sounds noble but usually just means, "I'm just not that into you."

We are so much better than that! You've got options, so let's break them down, shall we?

---

1. The Classic "Kind and Direct" Approach

You don't have to channel your inner Shakespeare to break the news. Sometimes, the best way to go about it is just to be straightforward. Rip off the Band-Aid, but with kindness and sincerity.

What to Say:

"Hey, I've enjoyed getting to know you, but I don't think we're romantically matched. You're great, but I think it's best to part ways before things get more serious. I wish you all the best!"

It's clear, respectful, and to the point—no emotional rollercoasters. This option is great if you're dealing with someone who can handle a little honesty—and bonus points if they appreciate your maturity.

Pro Tip: Think of this as a confidence boost. You're showing emotional intelligence by being upfront and cutting things off before they get complicated. Plus, you avoid ghosting (which again is only for friendly ghosts and Patrick Swayze).

---

2. The "Busy Bee" Option

If you're someone who prefers a gentle exit, the "I'm too busy" route can soften the blow while still making your point. This works well if they're nice people, but you don't feel the long-term potential.

What to Say:

"Hey! I've been thinking, and with everything going on in my life right now (work, hobbies, my never-ending quest to declutter my apartment), I don't think I'm in the right space to continue seeing each other. I've enjoyed our time together, but I need to focus on other things now."

Pro Tip: Use this option if you want to avoid a heavy emotional conversation but still want to offer a dignified exit. Ensure you're clear enough that they understand it's *over*—not just on a brief hiatus.

3. The "Keep It Light" Strategy

If you've only been on a couple of dates and the vibe has been super casual, you don't necessarily need to launch into a heartfelt breakup speech. Sometimes, it's okay to keep things breezy.

What to Say:
"This has been fun, but I'm not feeling a deeper connection. I think it's best if we call it here. I'm sure you'll find someone great soon—good luck out there!"

Short, sweet, and to the point. This option works best when both of you haven't invested much emotional energy and the situation is casual enough that a light-hearted exit won't feel too abrupt.

Pro Tip: Make sure your tone matches the casual nature of the message. This works best when things haven't gotten too serious yet, and both of you are still in the "getting to know you" phase.

---

4. The "Silver Lining" Technique

Let's be real—sometimes, you must give them *something* to soften the blow. The silver lining approach gives a compliment while still delivering the message that you're moving on.

What to Say:
"You're really funny/interesting/kind, and I've enjoyed hanging out. But I'm realizing I don't see us as a romantic match. I know you'll find someone who really appreciates you, and I wish you all the best!"

Flattery never hurts—especially when it's paired with a graceful exit. This approach works when you want to credit them for being an awesome person (just not *your* awesome person).

Pro Tip: Use this when you want to leave things on a genuinely positive note. It's not about false compliments—it's about highlighting their strengths while still stepping away. It keeps things respectful but clear.

Empower Yourself: You Deserve to Feel Confident in Saying No

At the end of the day, telling someone you're not interested is about respecting both your feelings and theirs. You're not doing anyone any favors by dragging things out when you know it's not working. Saying "no" is empowering—it shows that you're clear on what you want (and don't want), and that's a major win.

You're allowed to step away from situations that don't feel right, even if the person is nice or the dates have been fun. You deserve to feel a spark, be excited, and be fully invested in your connections. If that's not happening, it's time to gracefully exit. You're not being selfish or "too picky" by walking away. You're being honest. And that's the best gift you can give someone when things aren't clicking.

Story Time: The Breakup That Wouldn't Stick: Pedicures, Lunch Dates, and Wedding RSVPs

Let me take you back to a time when I thought I was being mature, direct, and completely reasonable—only to have it blow up in the most bizarre yet weirdly generous way.

So, I was dating this guy—let's call him Damon. Nice enough guy, sweet, but after a couple of months, it became clear that we were on very *different* pages. While I was in the "let's take things slow and see where it goes" chapter, Damon had already skipped ahead to "this is my soulmate, let's get matching sweaters and plan Thanksgiving with my parents in Connecticut page." I will freely admit during that time in my life, the word commitment made me nauseous, and the idea of being on a Costco membership with someone would make me faint, but this guy was going from 0 to 100. We had been talking for 2 months, and we were not exclusive.

To give you an idea: on date three, he asked me if I was more of a big wedding or a small ceremony on a beach with only friends and family person. We were moving at breakneck speed, and I was still trying to figure out if I liked spending time with him.

Realizing that this wasn't working, I decided to do the right thing. I sat him down for *the talk*. I told him that, while he was a great guy, I wasn't ready for things to move this fast. I was kind and clear, and I even let him know that I was not the marrying type (Refer to book number 2's title). And to his credit, Damon *seemed* to understand. He nodded, thanked me for being honest, and said he respected my decision. Easy, right? Problem solved. I was free, and that knot in my stomach was gone!

Or so I thought.

Exactly one week later, I'm at work—just minding my own business and living my best single life—when Damon strolls in with a giant bag of takeout like we are still in the honeymoon phase. *"I thought you might like some lunch,"* he said, with the kind of casual confidence that suggested he'd *completely* forgotten we had broken up. The awkwardness set in immediately.

"Uh, thanks… but didn't we…" I started, gently reminding him of the conversation we'd just had. Before I could finish, he waved me off, grinning like a Labrador Retriever.

"Oh, I know. I just figured, you know, we're still friends, right? And friends, bring each other lunch."

Friends? Did he not hear the *breakup* part? I thanked him awkwardly, accepted the food (because, well, free lunch), and figured that would be the end of it.

It wasn't.

Two days later, I got a notification on my phone: *Damon has just sent you $50 on Venmo.* The message? "For a pedicure. Thought you'd like to treat yourself!" Don't get me wrong—I'm not one to turn down a pedicure fund—but we were broken up. *Broken. Up.*

I texted him a polite "Thank you, but you don't need to do this," to which he replied, "I know I don't need to, but I *want* to." The red flags were flapping in the wind at this point, but I naively thought (I was also a very poor grad student, which doesn't make it right, but just giving full context here), "Hey, at least he's being nice about it."

But then, things took an even weirder turn.

My sister texted me a few days later, saying, "Hey, did you know Damon bought five squares in my kid's school fundraiser?" Apparently, this man—whom I had clearly ended things with—had tracked down my nephew's fundraiser page and bought multiple squares as if we were still happily dating and heading to a PTA meeting together. The man spent 250 dollars for my nephew's class to go to science camp. I started to feel like I was in a romantic comedy without any romance.

The final straw came when I got a message from Damon, which seemed innocent enough at first: *"Hey, what is your favorite color?"* I replied, *"Green,"* to which he said, *"It isn't my best color, but I guess I can make it work."* Confused, I asked, *"What now?"* He replied, *"I was just wondering what color you'll be wearing for my cousin's wedding in July."* Mind you, this was **two months after we had broken up**. July. As in, post-breakup, Damon was now envisioning me as his date to a family wedding four months from now (for those not great at math, that is 6 months after I had thought I ended things).

I stared at my phone for a solid minute, wondering if I had somehow slipped into an alternate universe where "breakup" meant "see you at family functions." At that point, I realized I needed to have a *second* breakup talk—because, apparently, the first one didn't stick.

I kindly reminded him (again) that we had broken up and that buying lunch, sending pedicure money, spending money on my nephew's fundraiser, and RSVPing me to his cousin's wedding was not part of the plan. He responded with, "Oh, I just thought we were still, you know, hanging out."

Hanging out? Hanging out is what you do with your friends, not someone who explicitly told you they were moving on.

I finally had to draw the line with a very direct (but kind) message: "Damon, I think it's time we stop the lunches, the money, and the fundraisers. I really need to move on, and I think it's best if we don't stay in touch anymore."

Thankfully, that did the trick. And while I never got to enjoy that wedding with him (shocker, I know), I did walk away with a wild story, a free pedicure, and the undeniable knowledge that some breakups require a second round of clarity.

Story Time part Deux: From Heartbreak to Happily Ever After— A Friendship That Survived the Swipe

---

Now, not all break-up stories are as awkward or drawn out. Breaking up is never easy, especially when you genuinely like someone and things seem to be going well. But sometimes, life throws curveballs in the form of incompatible schedules and different lifestyles. Let me take you back to a time when I had to respectfully part ways with someone who was nothing short of wonderful.

We had been seeing each other for about a month, enjoying each other's company and building a nice connection. She had a low-stress job, working less than 30 hours a week, which made her seem like the perfect balance to my whirlwind 80-hour work weeks. At first, it felt like we complemented each other beautifully—she brought calm and relaxation into my hectic life, and I, in turn, introduced her to the excitement of my fast-paced world.

As the weeks went by, she started feeling like I wasn't putting enough time into our relationship. Even though we had agreed to keep things casual, her feelings were growing, and I could sense her frustration. I tried to ramp up my communication, squeezing in more time whenever possible, but it wasn't enough to bridge the gap between our vastly different schedules.

Eventually, I realized that our lifestyles were just not compatible. It wasn't about not liking each other; it was about the practicalities of our lives clashing in ways that couldn't be ignored. After some heartfelt conversations, we decided to part ways amicably. Both of us were bummed, but deep down, we knew it was the right choice.

To our mutual relief, we agreed to stay friends, preserving the good memories without the added pressure of a mismatched relationship.

Fast forward three years, I found myself sitting at her wedding as a guest, surrounded by her friends and family, celebrating her new chapter. As the toasts began, each person shared how they knew the brides, and when it was my turn, I couldn't help but chuckle before saying, "We're old friends."

Seeing her smile and knowing that our decision to part ways had allowed us to maintain a meaningful friendship and also allowed her to meet the love of her life was incredibly rewarding. It was a beautiful reminder that sometimes, letting go of a romantic relationship can lead to something just as valuable—an enduring friendship that stands the test of time.

Pro Tip: Not every relationship is meant to be a forever romance. Sometimes, recognizing incompatibilities and choosing to remain friends can lead to lasting and fulfilling connections. My Grandma Pearl always said people are meant to come into your life, some for a short time and some for a long time." Embrace the friendships that survive the dating drama—they often enrich your life.

There you have it—a guide to letting someone down with kindness, wit, and just enough finesse to keep it respectful. Remember, rejection doesn't have to be painful, and being upfront is a form of self-respect (and also shows respect for them). So, put on your best smile, take a deep breath, and know you've handled things like an absolute boss.

Chapter 12

The Fine Art of Juggling Multiple Dates Without Dropping the Ball (or Your Sanity)

So, you've swiped right on more than one person (okay, more like five), and suddenly, you're out here in full-on dating juggle mode. Congratulations! You've entered the wild and wonderful world of multi-dating. But here's the thing—dating multiple people isn't just about cramming your calendar full of happy hours and coffee meet-ups. It's about balancing personalities, keeping stories straight, and—most importantly—doing it all *ethically*.

I try to be as honest with you, dear reader, as I possibly can. At my peak, I had a roster; yes, I said roster of 14. I know some of you need time to re-read that sentence or pick your jaw up off the floor, but it can be done. I was open with all of the people I was seeing. Some were in the stages of getting to know one another, and others were a little more serious. I did this while holding five jobs, four book clubs, two women's groups, and a needy dog named Oso. That is not a brag; actually, it is a little because damn... go me, huh? Or maybe I need to talk with my therapist about my need to overplan my life. But really, it is to say there is nothing wrong with playing the field, and you can do it in a sexy and ethical way. So, here's how to juggle multiple dating prospects without accidentally calling someone by the wrong name or turning your love life into a circus act.

1. Honesty is Sexy (and Ethical)

First things first—let's talk about honesty. The last thing you want to be is *that person* who leads multiple people on, acting like each is the only one. That's not juggling; that's just setting yourself up for a romantic disaster (with a side of guilt). Being upfront about your intentions is the key to juggling dates like a boss. You don't need to send a mass text message to your "roster" saying, "I'm dating three other people," or give everyone your exact dating schedule, but you *do* need to clarify that you're keeping things casual and seeing multiple people.

What to Say: "I'm having fun getting to know people right now, and I'm not rushing into anything serious. I am seeing other people. I just wanted to be upfront so we're on the same page."

It's honest and sexy and shows you're in control of your dating life without pretending to be exclusive. Plus, it sets the expectation that no one's jumping into a commitment after date two.

---

2. Keep It Straight: Names, Stories, and Important Details

Let's face it—if you're seeing multiple people, keeping their stories, quirks, and fun facts straight is a *full-time job*. The last thing you want is to mix up someone's dog's name with their kids' name, confuse who's training for a marathon, or accidentally ask someone about a hobby that belongs to someone else. Cue the awkward silence.

One of the easiest ways to keep track of who's who is to put their details, where you met or have gone on dates, their quirks, etc., right in your phone. No more "Antonio #3" or "Sara Bumble." It's time to label them with something that reminds you of them.

What to Do: Add them into your contacts with a little descriptor that jogs your memory:

- "Brad—Loves Horror Movies, Terrified of Clowns"
- "Sophia—Yoga Instructor, Dog: Mr. Sprinkles"
- "Alex—Baker, Obsessed with Travel"

Not only does this help you avoid those cringe-worthy moments when you can't remember who loves sushi and who hates it, but it also makes it way easier to craft personal messages. "How's Mr. Sprinkles doing?" will score way more points than "How's…uh, your dog?"

Pro Tip: If you're really dating at pro-level status, take notes after dates. It sounds a little ridiculous, but trust me, it works. You don't need a whole spreadsheet (unless that's your jam, and if so, love that for you), but jotting down key details can save you from those awkward "wait, did I tell you this already?" moments.

3. Time Management: Because You Should Still Have a Life

Multi-dating is fun, but it's also time-consuming. If you're not careful, your entire calendar will be full of dates, and you'll forget what it's like to have a night with some good TV and a face mask or a night out with friends. I have talked with many people who get frustrated with friends because they feel abandoned once their friends get into a relationship or start seriously dating. Make sure to have balance. So, how do you manage your time without burning out or double-booking yourself?

The Golden Rule of Multi-Dating: Don't over-schedule. Three dates a week? Sure. Three dates in *one* day? Hard pass. You don't want to be sprinting from one happy hour to the next, mixing up people's names and wondering why you're *this* close to Googling "Where are we at with cloning?" I once had seven dates in a day! Four zero dates and three real ones. I was a literal zombie by the end, and it was unfair to all parties involved.

Practical Tip: Use your calendar. Seriously, schedule your dates like you would anything else. It'll save you from accidentally agreeing to see two people on the same night (awkward), ensuring you have some precious "me time" in between. Plus, spacing things out lets you enjoy each date instead of feeling like you're speed-dating across town. Block off "rest days" on your calendar. You're juggling, not joining a dating marathon. Give yourself time to recharge so you don't show up to date number three with the emotional energy of a soggy pancake.

---

4. Keep Things Light (Until You Want Them Heavy)

When you're dating multiple people, it's easy to feel like you're juggling emotional grenades. Do they want something serious? Are they falling for you after three dates? Should you *want* something serious? Relax. It's okay to keep things light and casual as long as you're honest. You don't owe anyone a grand plan for the future just because you've been out a few times.

What to Say: "I'm really enjoying getting to know you, but I'm not rushing to define things just yet. Let's keep having fun and see where it goes!"

This lets them know you're into them and keeps the vibe fun and relaxed. You're not signing a contract, and you're certainly not promising to pick out curtains together at IKEA.

5. Know When to Focus In

At some point, one of these casual connections might stand out. Maybe you find yourself thinking about them a little more than the others, or you realize you'd rather spend your Friday night with them rather than juggling two other dates. When that happens, it's time to make a decision: do you keep juggling, or is it time to focus?

What to Do: Be honest with yourself and the people you're dating. If one person is starting to stand out, it might be time to either focus on them or at least have a conversation about where things are going. If you're ready to take things more seriously with one person, let the others down gently. No need to ghost—just let them know it's been fun, but you're ready to move forward with someone else.

6. Keep It Fun (But Don't Be a Jerk)

Juggling multiple dates can be sexy, fun, and totally empowering—but it's not a game. It's easy to slip into player mode when you're texting three different people at once, but remember that you're dealing with real humans who deserve respect. Be kind and ensure no one gets hurt just because you're having fun.

You can keep things light, casual, and sexy without playing games or leading people on. Just because you're dating more than one person doesn't mean you're a heartbreaker—it just means you're exploring your options. And there's nothing wrong with that if you do it correctly.

Story Time: Rumspringa Gone Wrong: The 7-Date Juggling Act

Let's rewind a bit, shall we? Not too long ago, I was fresh out of a relationship with someone I genuinely thought was my "Person." We'd spent three years "building" a life together, which included me pouring blood, sweat, and a few choice swear words into rehabbing a house that clearly had more issues than a reality show cast. If that wasn't enough fun, my ex made not-so-subtle suggestions that I rearrange my entire social calendar to fit his vision of what "mother and wife material" looked like. I'm talking major life edits here: curb the late-night shenanigans, dial down the happy hours, and maybe pick up knitting or something equally domestic. Spoiler alert: I'm about as good at "toning down" as a peacock is at hiding its tail feathers.

So yeah, when that whole fantasy went up in a puff of questionable paint fumes and broken promises, I was done. Done with trying to mold myself into someone else's idea of what a proper partner should be. I was done with the carrot-dangling and the "maybe next year we'll get serious" speeches. I packed up both my physical and emotional baggage and walked away. It felt like I'd just escaped a very beige, very boring cult.

Enter my personal Rumspringa—a concept I stole right out of Amish tradition, minus the butter churning and barn dances. In my interpretation, Rumspringa meant going on as many dates as humanly possible, leaning shamelessly into the "Yes" button on every invitation, and seeing what kind of glorious, messy life I could lead without all that compromise and expectation stuff. No bonnets, no fields of wheat—just me, a calendar that looked like a complicated Sudoku puzzle, and a serious caffeine habit. I was basically running my own pop-up version of "The Bachelorette" every single day.

Here's where my well-meaning but slightly deranged over-planning side comes into play. Where most people's Rumspringa involves spontaneous road trips, mine involved color-coded Google calendars and carefully timed escape routes. In a single day, I booked not one, not two, but seven dates. Seven! There were so many suitors, so few hours, and a whole lot of coffee standing between me and a total meltdown.

The strategy was bulletproof—on paper, anyway. I had four "Zero Dates," which is basically shorthand for low-stakes, quick-and-dirty get-to-know-you meet-ups. A coffee meetup for that morning jolt, a romp through my favorite bookstore (where I could judge them by their reading tastes, obviously), a park stroll to observe humans in their semi-natural habitat, and a casual drink that could quickly be upcycled into a full evening if they played their cards right. Between those, I'd stuffed in three "Real Dates": breakfast with a charmer who appreciated early morning eggs as much as I did, a bowling-and-booze combo to test their sense of humor and tolerance for public embarrassment, and, finally, a dinner date with a woman I'd been seeing for a bit who deserved my slightly less caffeinated presence.

Now, if you're wondering how I survived this emotional game of Twister, let me tell you: with a grin, a lot of eyeliner, and a quick prayer to Alanis Morissette (If you do not know, she plays God in Dogma and it is amazing. Again, if you have not seen that movie, what have you been doing with your life? Please pause here and watch it so this joke can land). On the coffee date, I learned my suitor had been "politely asked to leave" multiple pubs because he was a "wild card" (insert eyebrow raised here). I mentally bookmarked him as a "friend or emergency contact if I ever needed to escape a dull party." On the park date, we saw a dog dressed as a bumblebee, which was a surprisingly great conversation starter:

we ended up debating the psychological underpinnings of people who treat pets like human toddlers. At the bowling alley, after three gutter balls, I shrugged theatrically and joked about me throwing the game so they could feel superior for once, securing a laugh that teetered between "she's charming" and "she might have issues, but let's roll with it."

By the time I reached the dinner date—I felt like a marathon runner staggering toward the finish line, sweaty but determined. I was practically patting myself on the back. I'd orchestrated a delicate ballet of romantic possibilities and managed to emerge relatively unscathed. Bravo, me! Let's clink glasses and toast to my newfound freedom, shall we?

That's when fate decided to bitch slap me. Across the bar, I spotted him: Coffee Date Guy. Yes, the first date of the day, the one who hated rap music with the passion of a thousand scorned DJs. He was glaring at me like I'd just crashed his grandmother's birthday party. Before I could avert my eyes or feign a seizure, he approached, wearing the smuggest grin this side of the Mississippi.

"Good to see you again," he said, voice dripping with gotcha sweetness. "Didn't realize everyone got a date with you today."

Oh, bless him. He thought this would shame me. He didn't realize I'd just survived a dating obstacle course like I was training for the Olympics of Singlehood. I had three options: pretend I'd lost my hearing, throw my drink in his face for dramatic effect, or own it like the queen I am.

I smiled like he'd just paid me the nicest compliment. "What can I say? I'm an overachiever. Besides, you got me first this morning, so you are welcome. If you have further complaints, I would take it up with our HR department.

He blinked. My dinner date looked like she was trying hard not to spit out her drink. And just like that, Coffee Date Guy realized he wasn't going to win this duel of wits. With a forced nod, he retreated to whatever corner of the bar he crawled out of.

As soon as he was gone, my date burst out laughing. "Wow," she said, eyes sparkling, "that's what happens when you run a dating marathon?"

I shrugged with the kind of well-rehearsed indifference that only comes after surviving seven back-to-back dates and one too many double espressos. "It's not pretty," I said, raising my glass, "but someone's got to do it."

The moral of the story? Let's just say that my Rumspringa taught me a valuable lesson about pacing, honesty, and the power of a well-timed comeback. Seven dates in one day might seem like a brilliant adventure at first, but trust me—when you're playing the dating field like a hyper-caffeinated Robin Hood of affections, someone's bound to call you out. And honestly? If you're going to get caught, you might as well get caught looking fabulous with a witty retort on the tip of your tongue.

Final Thoughts: Multi-Dating Like a Pro

So, there you have it—juggling multiple dates without losing your mind (or your morals). Be honest, stay organized, and, most importantly, *have fun*. Whether you're dating two people or 14 (hey, no judgment), as long as you're keeping things clear and ethical, you're doing it right.

And if all else fails, just remember—there's no shame in putting "Sushi Guy," "Yoga Girl," or "Guitar Person" in your phone to keep things straight.

Chapter 13

From Swipe Right to Sleep Tight: Moving From Casual Dating to Intimacy

So, you've been casually dating for a while now, and things are heating up. You've gone from flirty banter and playful touches to that all-important moment where the conversation is about to shift from "When's our next date?" to "When's our next *sleepover*?" Moving into intimacy is exciting, but it's also a time to get real about what you both want and need in the bedroom.

Before you dive between the sheets, let's get one thing straight: being intimate isn't just about physical connection—it's about feeling *empowered* to express your desires, needs, and boundaries. Because let's be honest, nothing kills the mood faster than miscommunication, awkward assumptions, or a crossed boundary. How many of us have had that moment where things get so weird, and the night and potentially the relationship is ruined? So, how do you go from casual to *crazy good* in bed? Let's break it down.

Create a Safe Space

Assure your partner that this is a judgment-free zone. You're sharing because you want to enhance your connection, not because you're dissatisfied. Likewise, be receptive to their desires without jumping to conclusions or judgments. **Trust and openness go both ways.**

1. Talk Dirty (But Make it Clear)

We're all for getting a little flirty, but before things start sizzling, it's time to hit pause for a quick reality check. Don't worry, this doesn't have to be an awkward, overly formal conversation with a PowerPoint presentation on boundaries and limits (though, if PowerPoint is your jam, hey, go for it). Think of it as setting the stage for an experience you'll both enjoy, with clear cues and no surprise plot twists; this is not an M. Night Shyamalan Movie. This is about real, open talk: what you like, what you're curious about, and what's absolutely, positively not on the menu.

What to Bring Up:

- **Likes and Dislikes:** What really gets you going? Are there certain things that just *do not* work for you? If you love slow, drawn-out moments, say it. If you've got off-limits places, be clear. No need to be coy. ("Stay away from my bellybutton and toes, Brad! Those are my no-no squares.") It's like highlighting the "do not touch" exhibits at a museum—you're keeping things clear and avoiding any accidental boundary-crossing. Now's your chance to set the scene for what you enjoy—and where you draw the line. Whether it's something as simple as "I love being kissed here" or "This particular thing isn't for me," this talk keeps both of you in sync. Think of it like GPS for your night in—it's your roadmap to avoid awkward detours, unnecessary U-turns, and the dreaded "Um, what are you doing?" moment.

- **Protection:** This is a non-negotiable and doesn't have to be an awkward conversation. Have the condom talk, discuss birth control, and get real about sexual health. After all, nothing kills the mood faster than an "Oh, by the way…" mid-action. You can keep it light and still make sure you're protected. Remember, responsibility is sexy—plus, it shows you respect yourself and your partner.

- **Screening and Testing:** I'm a big proponent of regular testing and think everyone should be, too. Many people wildly under-test and leave a lot to chance, and let's be real—symptoms don't always make themselves known. So, make a plan, stay informed, and consider it a health check-in for everyone's peace of mind. It's a must for me, but I'll leave that for you to decide. Think of it like getting your car inspected before a road trip—you want to know everything's good to go before you take it cross-country.

Spicy Tip: Make this conversation part of the fun. There's no rule saying these topics must be boring or clinical. Start with playful flirting about what's been on your mind lately, then ease into the practical stuff. In fact, plenty of fun card games and board games are designed to bring up these topics in a light, playful way. These games and conversations can add extra heat while building comfort and anticipation.

Think of this conversation as an invitation, not a restriction. You're creating a space where you both feel safe and excited, where expectations are clear, and where you can fully enjoy each other's company without the potential for awkward moments or crossed wires. And remember, confidence is key—there's nothing more appealing than someone who knows what they do and don't want and communicates it clearly.

There's nothing sexier than confidence, especially when it comes to expressing what you want between the sheets—or wherever your adventures take you. This is your chance to be upfront about what makes you feel good, what turns you on, and what makes you feel safe. Don't shy away from owning your desires—whether they're kinky, romantic, or completely new territories you're eager to explore. Remember, vulnerability can be incredibly empowering.

Think of it this way: if you don't tell them you love dark chocolate with sea salt, how are they supposed to surprise you with your favorite treat? The same goes for intimacy. Your partner is no Professor Xavier, so they cannot read your mind (If you do not get that reference, please stop and watch at least the first two X-Men Movies. If for nothing else, to see Halle Berry in Spandex).

Confidence isn't just about knowing what you want—it's about feeling comfortable enough to communicate it. Whether you've been dreaming about a slow, sensual evening or curious about trying that intriguing idea you read about, now's the time to bring it up. After all, closed mouths don't get fed.

Communication is a Two-Way Street

Remember, being intimate is a two-way street, and the road is much smoother when both parties are vocal about their desires and boundaries. Don't assume your partner knows what you're thinking—they're likely juggling their own thoughts and maybe even a few insecurities. **The best intimacy happens when both people feel comfortable and excited to satisfy each other.**

Encourage an open dialogue. Ask them what they like, what they've always wanted to try, or what makes them feel most connected. This enhances your physical connection and builds trust and emotional intimacy.

What to Say: Making the Conversation Natural

Not sure how to bring it up? Here are some conversation starters to keep things light and engaging:

- "I absolutely love it when you do [specific action]. I'd be really into trying [new thing] too—what do you think?"

Why it works: You compliment them while introducing a new idea, making it a positive and collaborative discussion.

- "I've been thinking about [insert fantasy], and I'm curious about what you've been dreaming of trying."

Why it works: You're sharing something personal and inviting them to do the same, fostering mutual vulnerability.

- "It feels incredible when you [fill in the blank]. Honestly, more of that would be amazing!"

Why it works: Positive reinforcement is always a good idea. It lets them know they're doing something right and boosts their confidence.

- "I read about [specific activity], which intrigued me. How would you feel about exploring that together?"

Why it works: You're introducing an external idea, which can make the suggestion feel less pressured and more like a time for exploration.

Spicy Tip: Turn Talk into Play

Pro Tip: Don't wait until the heat of the moment to bring these things up. Talking about what you both enjoy beforehand can make the experience easier and more fun. Plus, anticipation is half the excitement!

Make the conversation part of the fun:

- **Flirty Texting:** Send a playful message during the day hinting at what you'd like to do later. For example, "Can't stop thinking about that thing we talked about last night." This builds anticipation and opens the door for them to share their thoughts.

- **Game Night with a Twist:** Plenty of card games and board games are designed to spark intimate conversations and reveal desires in a light-hearted way. Games like "Monogamy," "Talk, Flirt, Dare," or even customized truth-or-dare can make sharing more fun.

- **Pillow Talk:** Use those quiet moments after intimacy to casually bring up what you enjoyed and what you'd love to try next time. The relaxed atmosphere can make it easier to open up.

Embrace the Awkward (If It Happens)

It's okay if the conversation initially feels awkward—that's completely normal. What's important is pushing through that initial discomfort to reach a place of openness. Laugh it off if you stumble over your words. Humor can be a great way to ease tension and show that you're human.

Final Thoughts

Confidence in expressing your desires leads to more fulfilling intimacy and strengthens your overall relationship. Being clear and open sets the foundation for trust, respect, and mutual satisfaction.

So go ahead, speak up, ask questions, and dive into those conversations with enthusiasm. Your willingness to communicate can turn good experiences into unforgettable ones.

---

2. Take It Slow—or Not: Finding Your Perfect Pace

Let's dive deeper. Intimacy isn't about sprinting to the finish line but enjoying the journey. The excitement often lies in the build-up—the lingering glances, the accidental touches, the shared laughter over inside jokes. Taking your time allows both of you to fully immerse yourselves in the experience, building a connection that's both physical and emotional.

Sure, you're both eager to get to the fun stuff, but intimacy is often better when it's not rushed. Take your time if you're still figuring out each other's vibes. Build up the anticipation. A well-timed slow burn is way sexier than jumping into things too quickly and having an awkward moment.

However, I'm a big believer in "test-driving before you buy." Some people prefer to hold off on sex until they're in a committed relationship, and that's totally valid. No shade to them! But I do believe that an intimate connection is crucial to the success of a relationship, and sometimes it's just not there between two people, no matter how perfect things seem on paper.

Sometimes, you need to know if that *spark* is there sooner rather than later. Physical compatibility is a significant part of any romantic relationship. You can have matching playlists, synchronized Netflix queues, and a mutual love for Thai takeout, but if the chemistry fizzles in the bedroom, it can throw a wrench in the whole operation.

I've had my fair share of experiences where everything aligned perfectly on paper—we're talking about shared hobbies, having great conversations, and the whole nine yards. But when it came down to it, the fireworks were more like sparklers—cute but not exactly lighting up the sky. It's like baking a cake with all the right ingredients but ending up with a loaf of bread. Close, but not quite what you were aiming for.

Finding the Right Tempo

The key here is communication and mutual understanding. Maybe you both want to take things slow and enjoy the courtship dance. Or perhaps you're on the same page about fast-tracking the physical connection to see if that elusive chemistry exists. Either way, it's about finding a rhythm that suits both of you.

Spicy Strategies:

- **Flirt Like It's an Olympic Sport**: Send cheeky texts, drop hints about what you'd like to do together, or share a funny meme that captures your mood. Building that tension can make the eventual payoff that much sweeter.

- **Plan Teaser Dates:** Go on outings that allow for closeness without the pressure. Think salsa dancing classes (hello, built-in excuses to touch) or cooking a meal together (food fights optional but encouraged).

- **Communicate Openly:** Don't be shy about discussing your desires and expectations. If you're eager to move things along, express that. If you'd prefer to pump the brakes, let them know. Honesty is the best policy—and a major turn-on.

- **Experiment Together:** If you're already physically intimate, take the time to explore each other's preferences. Slow down the pace, try new things, and pay attention to the details. Sometimes, it's the little tweaks that make all the difference.

Timing Is Everything—and Nothing

Timing can be a fickle friend. You might meet someone amazing when one of you isn't ready to dive into something serious, or perhaps external factors complicate things. It's important to recognize that while timing can influence a relationship, it doesn't have to dictate it entirely.

Final Thoughts:

Whether you choose to take the scenic route or the express lane, the most important thing is that both of you are comfortable and enthusiastic about the pace. There's no universal right or wrong here—just what's right for *you*. Embrace the journey, be open to where it leads, and remember that sometimes the best connections happen when you let go of expectations and simply enjoy the moment.

So go ahead, tease a little, laugh a lot, and don't be afraid to test-drive that potential partnership. After all, life's too short for what-ifs and missed opportunities. And who knows? You might find that the less traveled road leads to destinations beyond your wildest dreams.

3. Get Practical: The Little Things Matter

We all know that intimacy isn't just about what happens *in* the bedroom—it's about how you set the stage. Think about the environment, the mood, and the little details that can take things from "eh" to "oh yes." Whether it's the right music, lighting, or even keeping things like lube and protection within arm's reach, small things can make a big difference.

What to Think About:

- **Setting the mood:** Lighting, music, and ambiance all help create the right vibe. Dim the lights, pick a playlist that gets you both in the mood, and create a space where you can relax and focus on each other.

- **Bring the essentials:** Lube, protection, and anything else you might need to make the experience smooth and seamless. There's nothing less sexy than interrupting the flow to dig through a drawer for something you could've had ready.

- **Stay present:** Once you're in the moment, stay there. Put your phone on silent, clear your mind, and focus on each other. The best connections happen when you're fully present.

- **Get out of your head:** Too often, we are in our head about what they may be thinking, what our ex felt like if we shaved our big toe (You didn't. You never do). It is easy to get lost and miss out on what is happening right in front of us. There is nothing less sexy than looking at a partner that you know is thinking about something else instead of worshipping your perfect body.

4. Aftercare: Because Intimacy Doesn't End When Your Orgasm Does

Aftercare is often overlooked but can be one of the most important parts of intimacy, especially when you're moving from casual dating to something deeper. It's not just about cuddling, although that's great too. Aftercare is about checking in, making sure both people feel good, and staying connected *after* the main event. It shows respect and that you're invested in more than just the physical connection.

What to Do:

- "How are you feeling? What did you enjoy the most?"
- "Is there anything that you needed more or less of?"
- Cuddle, talk, and make sure you both feel good about the experience.
- Keep the connection alive after the moment has passed—whether sharing a laugh, staying in bed, or grabbing a drink together afterward.

Story Time: The Time I Was Almost Seduced by Seabiscuit

Let me tell you about the time I learned that not all "freaky" is created equal. It started like any other casual dating situation—we'd been seeing each other for a while, and things had gotten intimate a few times. Honestly, it was pretty good. So, when he asked if I was "freaky," I thought, *Hell yes, I'm freaky*. I was ready for whatever he had in mind.

That's when things got weird.

One night, after a few drinks and some flirty banter, he asked if I'd be into trying something a little... different. I've never been one to shy away from spicing things up, so I was all ears. When I asked him in a sultry voice to tell me about what he wanted to do to me, he said he wanted to tie me up and *show* me what *he* was into. The chemistry had been solid up to that point, and I figured, *What's the harm?* So, I agreed.

I put on some sexy lingerie, the kind that makes you feel like you own the room, and he tied me up to a chair with some cloth rope. It was tight enough to give some pressure but not so tight that I could escape if things went south. Blindfold on, anticipation building, I was ready for whatever wild, sexy ride he had in store. Cue *Genuine's "Pony"* playing in the background. You know the song—the ultimate "sexy time" anthem. I'm thinking, *Okay, he's into lap dances. A little Magic Mike action? I can work with that.*

The music was just getting into the groove, and I was bracing myself for the sexy moves I thought were coming. And then... I heard it.

"Neigh." KLOP... "Neigh"

Wait, what?

At first, I thought maybe it was a joke. A playful sound effect to lighten the mood. Then I heard it again— *"Neigh, neigh,"* followed by what could only be described as the sound of hooves clopping on the floor. Was I losing it? I felt like I was in my own version of Monty Python and the Holy Grail meets Showgirls (I feel like this is redundant, but if you have not watched either of these films, first of all, shame on you! Never seen the Holy Grail? A travesty! Go watch them, then come right back to this spot and think about how weird it would be if those two movies were spliced together with Ginuwine as the soundtrack. Now, with that scene set, let's get back to it, shall we?)

But no, it wasn't the tequila playing tricks on me. And boy, did I need about three more shots. The man I was tied up for, in what I thought was about to be the freakiest, most erotic night ever, was *making horse noises*. I mean, *full-on Seabiscuit performing an opera.*

It gets better—or worse, depending on how you look at it. I heard some rustling, and the next thing I knew, he was clomping around the room like he was in the Kentucky Derby. I whipped off my blindfold (because, let's be real, I needed to see this for myself), and sure enough, there he was, prancing around... in a *full-on horse costume*. Not just any horse costume—a legit furry suit, complete with a tail and a mane. I will give the man credit that this costume did look expensive, like he went all out on this thing, and he could be an extra in an old Western.

I sat there, tied up in sexy lingerie, watching this grown man gallop around the room like he was preparing for a big race. Suddenly, "Pony" wasn't so much a sexy song as it was the *soundtrack to my nightmare* and his hype music before a race.

I'm all for letting people express their kinks—truly, no judgment—but nowhere in my freaky rule book did I sign up for a private rodeo show. And this man? He was fully committed to his role as Seabiscuit, making neighing noises, trotting around like he was ready to cross the finish line. This man was 6'6 on his hands and knees, bucking, neighing, and moaning.

At this point, I had to take control of the situation (well, as much control as one can have when tied to a chair).

"Okay, I think I'm good on the whole Seabiscuit thing," I said. I was trying to sound casual, but my brain was screaming, *WHAT IS HAPPENING?!*

He paused mid-gallop, looking genuinely confused. "Wait, you're not into this? I thought you were up for anything."

I blinked. Was this man seriously asking if I wanted to get freaky with him in *a horse costume?*

"No," I said firmly, "I'm not into Seabiscuit. Thanks, though."

He looked disappointed, but honestly, I was too busy figuring out how I'd gotten from "freaky fun" to *the live-action version of Spirit: Stallion of the Cimarron.*

After a slightly awkward untangling process (which, let's be real, was the least awkward part of the evening at that point), I gathered my dignity and made it clear that this particular race had ended.

I left, not scarred exactly, but definitely with a newfound understanding of the phrase, *"Not all freaky is the same."* Lesson learned: the next time someone asks if I'm freaky, I'm following up with *clarifying questions*—because apparently, "freaky" can mean anything from light bondage to getting it on with Mr. Ed. If you are into the latter, you must read my 7th book, "Tie Me Up and Call Me Seabiscuit: The Book of Unconventional Desires."

And in case you're wondering—no, we did not go for round two. I can confidently say that Seabiscuit and I rode off into different sunsets.

Final Thoughts: Confidence is Sexy, Communication is Everything

The shift from casual dating to intimacy is an exciting milestone filled with possibility, vulnerability, and a lot of discovery. But here's the secret sauce: confidence and communication. Being upfront about your desires, limits, and curiosities doesn't just set the stage for a great intimate connection but deepens the emotional bond between you and your potential partner. After all, the best intimacy is built on mutual respect, understanding, and a shared sense of excitement.

Embrace Empowerment
Owning your desires is a form of self-love. When you ask for what you want and communicate your needs, you're telling both yourself and your partner that you're worth it—that your comfort, pleasure, and happiness matter. Confidence in intimacy isn't about being perfect or even "knowing it all"; it's about being unafraid to show up exactly as you are, quirks and everything. There's nothing sexier than being your authentic self, and in the context of intimacy, it can be a total game-changer.

Communication is the Ultimate Aphrodisiac
While physical attraction is often what draws people together, communication is what keeps the spark alive. Clear, honest dialogue isn't just a nice-to-have—it's essential. Expressing what you need, listening to what your partner desires, and being open to adjustments create intimacy far beyond the physical. A simple "What do you like?" or "How does this feel?" can make all the difference, turning a good experience into a truly memorable one.

A Few Last Words of Wisdom
Remember, there's no script for intimacy. Every relationship is unique, and what works for one couple may look entirely

different for another. So, embrace the adventure, talk openly, laugh often, and be gentle with each other. Be bold in expressing your needs, gracious in hearing theirs, and never underestimate the power of a well-placed compliment or a shared inside joke. These little things weave a connection that goes beyond words.

In the end, dating is less about finding someone perfect and more about finding someone whose imperfections mesh hilariously with your own. So, here's to the late-night conversations, the shared appetizers, and the mutual agreement that mint does not belong in ice cream or cookies. It belongs in toothpaste and Juleps (or does—we don't judge). Keep being authentically, unapologetically you—because that's the kind of confidence that doesn't just light up a room; it lights up someone's world.

Chapter 14
Swipe Right for Spice—The Sexual Archetypes of Dating Apps

So now you have opened the door to becoming intimate with people you have met online. You have dived headfirst into the wild world of finding sexual partners from dating apps, and let me tell you—it's a real-life Pokémon situation out there. Everyone's got a "type," and trust me, you'll meet some *interesting* characters, each with their own sexy, intriguing, or downright puzzling archetypes. Whether they're into romantic candlelit dinners or full-on kink dungeon vibes, here's your field guide to the sexual archetypes you might encounter while swiping.

1. The "Romantic Poet"

They're here for soul-deep connections, writing long texts about "making love" and how they want to stare into your eyes until dawn breaks. Expect roses, candlelit dinners, and dramatic pauses in bed. Think notebook, minus the rain and Ryan Gosling.

Signature Move: Eye contact that lingers far too long, paired with heartfelt quotes about love delivered at hilariously inappropriate moments—like when they're inside you.

2. The "Kink Aficionado"

Bio says "open-minded" and "sex positive" with a *wink* emoji. This one's ready to break out the handcuffs and give you a crash course in their extensive collection of toys. They're not here for vanilla anything. You'll know what you're getting into within the first ten minutes of chatting.

Signature Move: Asking about your comfort level with ropes before date two.

---

3. The "Fast-Forwarder"

This person wants to hit "skip intro" on the dating part and get straight to the fun. Think about late-night invites, flirty messages sent at 2 a.m., and zero interest in "getting to know you" beyond what they already see.

Signature Move: "You up?" texts at wildly inappropriate hours.

---

4. The "Vanilla King/Queen/Royalty"

Simple, sweet, and dependable. They're not looking for anything wild—just some classic, feel-good fun. Think cozy nights in the missionary position and lots of cuddling. No surprises here, but sometimes that's exactly what you need.

Signature Move: Suggesting Netflix and chilling and actually meaning it.

---

5. The "Overconfident Rockstar"

They're here to tell you exactly how good they are in bed. Their bio brags about all the "compliments" they've received, and they've probably got a shirtless mirror selfie thrown in for good measure. Spoiler: The talk usually outweighs the action.

Signature Move: Talking *a lot* about their "technique" and the fact that they can give references if you need them.

---

6. The "Explorer"

They're down for anything, and I mean *anything*. From tantric massage workshops to a casual make-out session at a random rooftop bar, this one's here to try it all. They're spontaneous and game for whatever, but don't expect consistency.

Signature Move: "Let's meet tonight and see where the night takes us..."

---

7. The "In-Depth Communicator"

This one's all about communication—*a lot* of it. They'll check in with you every five minutes to make sure you're comfortable, happy, hydrated, and okay with what's happening. They are super considerate, but sometimes you wish they'd just shut up and let you *enjoy the moment*.

Signature Move: "Is it good?" every two seconds.

---

8. The "Adventure Junkie"

Everything is a thrill with this one, from hiking to skydiving to pushing sexual boundaries. They live for adrenaline and want you along for the ride, whether a trek through the woods or a sexy game of truth or dare. Just don't expect a slow build-up—they're here for the *rush*.

Signature Move: Suggesting a hike *and* skinny-dipping for date one.

---

9. The "Intellectual Charmer"

For them, sex starts with the mind. They'll engage you in deep conversations about philosophy, art, or history before things get physical. You're out of the game if you can't keep up intellectually.

Signature Move: Debating the ethics of desire right before the first kiss.

---

10. The "Emotional Whirlwind"

This one gets attached *fast*. After one date, they're already dropping lines like, "I feel such a deep connection with you." It's all passion and fire in the beginning but buckle up because things get intense *real* quick.

Signature Move: Talking about "our future" after date two.

Story Time: The "Bedroom Expert" Who Wasn't

I'll never forget one of the biggest claims of sexual expertise I encountered on a dating app. I was swiping through profiles when I stumbled upon someone who exuded this whole "I know exactly how to make someone feel like the goddess they are" vibe in their bio. Intrigued and slightly amused, I exchanged some flirty messages, and before I knew it, I was convinced—this would be something memorable.

So, we met up. The date was fine—pleasant conversation, shared interests, and a chemistry that hinted at potential. But it was clear they were feeling themselves way more than I was. Their head was barely fitting through the door at that point. Still, I thought, "Okay, maybe their confidence will translate into something impressive later." Spoiler: it did not.

I decided that I didn't want to wait for the next date to move things forward. I am a woman with needs, and they were attractive, so I thought, "Let's go for it." The night ended in what can only be described as an awkward sequence of events. It felt like a cringeworthy comedy special (think Tony Hinchcliffe at a Trump Rally). This "sex god" couldn't figure out what to do with their hands—did they mean to be sensual, or were they auditioning for a role in a mime troupe? They fumbled with basic moves, each gesture more confused than the last, and spent half the time narrating what they were doing, like they were Morgan Freeman in *March of the Penguins*. "I am now placing my member in the slippery area. Is this satisfactory?" I felt like maybe I was abducted by aliens, and they were trying to converse using what they thought were American colloquialisms. It was as if someone had handed them an instruction manual and said, "Figure it out as you go."

Someone with a wildly active imagination clearly wrote their bio because reality was nowhere near what was advertised. It felt like being back in a sex education class, having to explain to a prepubescent teenager what their anatomy was and how mine was different from theirs. I awkwardly guided the experience, hoping that somehow, magically, things would improve. Instead, I was stuck in a bizarre mix of coaching and live demonstration, where nothing seemed to be resonating with them.

I left that night with a story I knew I'd be telling friends over drinks for months to come. The "sex god"? They were more like a nervous intern on their first day, fumbling through tasks they had no training for. As I walked away, I couldn't help but laugh at the absurdity of it all. Here I was, having just survived one of the most awkward encounters of my dating career, armed with nothing but a sense of humor and a newfound appreciation for clear communication.

Sometimes, despite all the confidence and grandiose promises, things just don't click. Timing is a fickle bitch, and chemistry isn't something you can schedule or plan for. The best advice? Trust your instincts, laugh off the awkward moments, and never take yourself too seriously. Because in the end, the stories that make you laugh the hardest are the ones you'll cherish the most.

So, if you ever come across someone who claims to be a bedroom expert but turns out to be more of a bewildered apprentice, just remember it's all part of the wild, unpredictable adventure of modern dating. Embrace the chaos, enjoy the stories, and keep swiping—metaphorically and literally, the next match could be your perfect dance partner.

Claiming Your Sexual Energy: Women Owning It

Alright, let's switch gears here. We've spent enough time laughing at people who overhype their sexual prowess—what about flipping the script and owning our sexual energy unapologetically? Because here's the deal: for far too long, women have been conditioned to downplay their desires, to be coy, to "go with the flow," or worse—to *fake it* just to protect someone else's ego. But guess what? We're done with that. The days of pretending, polite head-nodding, and fake "porno" moans (You know the type... it sounds like a high-pitched prepubescent girl stuck on repeat saying "Yes..OH..YEAH..") in the bedroom are officially *over*.

In today's dating world, more and more women are stepping up and claiming their right to express what lights them up and what turns them off. And that's exactly how it should be. Claiming your sexual energy isn't about putting on a performance or playing into anyone else's fantasy; it's about tapping into your own, feeling the power in it, and knowing you have every right to express it. This isn't about being "too much" or "not enough." It's about being exactly who you are, in and out of the bedroom.

Rocci's Empowerment Secret: Name Yo Business

Now, confession, dear reader, my vagina has a first name (really her own persona and the first name is not O.S.C.A.R), and it is BALBOA. My name is Rocci (Pronounced Rocky. My mom was a Stallone fan, and she had a Rumpelstiltskin deal with her drug dealer in the 80s; it's a whole thing), so my vagina needed a powerful name. She is a knockout; she goes 12 rounds, and when you get into the ring with her, you will walk away battered and bruised.

Side note, all women should name their vaginas. It gives them power and strength that I think they deserve, and you can also blame them for bad decisions that you make ("Balboa was in charge... It wasn't me.") Naming your genitals will be the inspiration for my 8th book "Crowning Jewels: Naming Your Bits and Owning Your Royalty."

When Balboa is not happy or satisfied, there is no hiding it on my face or in other parts of my body. I know this may be a foreign concept for you, my dear reader, so I thought I would support you by providing some ideas. This is essentially like finding your stripper name by putting the name of your first pet and the name of the street you grew up on together (Mine is actually Pugsley Sugar Pine... Not a showstopper, I know). Please use the information below to find the new name for your business.

First Letter Of Your First Name	First Letter Of Your Last Name
A - Cock	A - Muffin
B - Sparkle	B - Pie
C - Jelly	C - Cake
D - Glitter	D - Meat
E - Sex	E - Pocket
F - Pink	F - Chute
G - Pretty	G - Hole
H - Sweet	H - Poodle
I - Warm	I - Taco
J - Cutie	J - Pit
K - Bitch	K - Burger
L - Princess	L - Kitty
M - Golden	M - Tunnel
N - Candy	N - Truffle
O - Dazzle	O - Cave
P - Angel	P - Box
Q - Honey	Q - Pot
R - Rainbow	R - Pit
S - Devil	S - Snatch
T - Pixie	T - Flaps
U - Super	U - Mitten
V - Venus	V - Smuggler
W - Kid	W - Cookie
X - Glow	X - Sandwich
Y - Love	Y - Buffet
Z - Flower	Z - Factory

No More Faking It

Let's get one thing straight: there's no room for faking it in the modern dating world. If something's not working, *speak up*. If you know exactly what you like, ask for it unapologetically. There's nothing sexier than a person who knows their body and isn't afraid to communicate their needs. It's about creating an honest, open space where you're able to express what feels good and what doesn't without feeling like you have to tiptoe around someone else's ego.

Gone are the days of suffering through a subpar experience just to "keep them happy" or looking up at the ceiling fan, mentally putting together your to-do list for the rest of the day while silently asking yourself, "Are they done yet?" No more polite smiling while thinking that this person doesn't know their way around a Cadillac, let alone a clitoris. No more lying to spare someone's feelings. Real, satisfying intimacy comes from communication, and the right partner will appreciate your honesty because they know it's coming from a place of mutual respect and genuine desire.

Expressing your desires and boundaries shouldn't be a grand, dramatic conversation. It can be as simple as guiding your partner in the moment or letting them know what really gets you going. Be direct, and don't apologize for it. If someone's feelings are hurt by you saying, "A little more to the left," they're probably not the right person for you. A real partner will appreciate your openness and use it to improve the experience for both of you.

Here's the beauty of it: when you're upfront about what you want, not only does it improve your own experience, but it also creates space for them to be more open. It's a mutual give-and-take where both feel empowered to share and explore. That's intimacy—real intimacy that goes beyond just the physical.

Turning Up the Confidence Dial

Owning your sexual energy is like turning the volume up on your confidence dial. It's about knowing that your needs are valid, your boundaries are important, and your pleasure is non-negotiable. This is about you—your body, your desires, your experience. You're allowed to say "yes" to what excites you, "no" to what doesn't, and "hell, maybe" to the things you're curious about. Confidence is magnetic, and it shows when you're comfortable with yourself. You're no longer performing; you're just *being*.

Remember, real confidence doesn't need to be shouted from the rooftops or typed in all caps with exclamation points and have multiple eggplant and peach emojis!!!

Let's Toss Out the Double Standards

And can we please toss out the outdated double standards while we're at it? If men are allowed to be vocal and assertive about what they want, women should be just as empowered to do the same. Being bold, expressive, and even a little demanding about what feels good doesn't make you "too much." It makes you someone who knows her worth, is deeply connected to her own energy, and is not here to settle for anything less than amazing.

The Era of Owning It

So here's the takeaway: owning your sexual energy means being unapologetically you and demanding that your needs get met also. It means tuning into your body, trusting your instincts, and expressing your needs without hesitation. This is about embracing your power, voice, and right to feel amazing. No one else gets to set the rules here—*you do*. And there's nothing sexier than someone who knows exactly what they deserve and isn't afraid to ask for it.

So go ahead, own it, express it, and enjoy every second because there's nothing more powerful—or beautiful—than a woman who's unapologetically in charge of her own pleasure.

Optimistic End Note

So, the next time you're swiping through dating profiles and stumble upon someone proclaiming themselves the world's greatest lover—complete with a shirtless bathroom selfie and a bio that reads like a bad romance novel—maybe take it with a grain of salt and a hearty eye roll. After all, if they were truly that amazing, they'd probably be too busy making passionate love to update their dating profile.

Final Pro Tip: If you ever do meet the self-proclaimed "world's best lover," maybe suggest a friendly competition—you know, for science. Worst-case scenario, you get a good story out of it. Best-case? Well, we'll leave that to your imagination.

So, here's to you, the bold, the brave, the wonderfully imperfect daters of the world. Keep swiping, keep laughing, and remember: the right person will appreciate you for exactly who you are—a fabulous, confident human who's not afraid to own it. Cheers to making the dating world a little more genuine and a lot more fun!

Chapter 15

The Dating Dilemma—When You've Got Options and Need to Choose

Well, well, well... look at you! You've managed to do the impossible: you're actually dating more than one great person at a time. Who would've thought? It's like the dating gods finally decided to throw you a bone, and now you're stuck with the tricky decision of picking who to move forward with. A tragic situation, really.

But fear not, you can't keep juggling forever—unless you're training to join Cirque du Soleil. So, how do you choose the lucky winner who gets the grand prize (a.k.a. more of your precious time)? Relax! I've got you covered with a handy checklist that'll help you narrow it down while keeping it as lighthearted as a bad rom-com.

---

1. Do They Make You Laugh?

Here's the cold truth: hard pass if they don't make you laugh. Sure, maybe they're good-looking, smart, or have an impressive job, but are they funny? Because, let's be real, life is way too long to spend it with someone who doesn't make you snort-laugh at least once a week. Forget fancy dinners and deep conversations—give me someone who can turn a bad day around with a stupid meme any day.

Checklist Question:

- Who's the one that makes you laugh until you question your bladder control?
- Who turns every basic text into an inside joke?
- Do they find lightness in tough/challenging situations?
- Can they make fun of themselves?

2. Can You Be Your Weird Self Around Them?

You want someone who loves you for your quirks, not someone pretending to be okay with them. If you can't be your authentic, unfiltered self—whether it's singing off-key in the car or having a panic attack because they don't understand the brilliance of Schitt's Creek—what's the point? You need someone who *gets* you, not someone who tolerates you.

Checklist Question:

- Who lets you be your full, weird self without judgment or an intervention?
- Who hasn't made you feel like you need to dial down your crazy just to impress them?
- Do they accept you when you are at your worst?
- Do they let you shine in areas they do not?

3. How's the Communication?

We're not looking for psychic abilities here but solid communication. It's non-negotiable. Can they text without making you feel like you're pulling teeth? Do they actually listen or just wait for their turn to talk? If you've already had five dates and they've yet to ask how your day was, that's a red flag. Communication is sexy, people—let's make sure they've got it.

Checklist Question:

- Who's actually listening when you talk and not just pretending they're interested in your latest story about the weird thing your coworker did?

- Who can text without sending you the dreaded "K"? (No one needs that kind of negativity.)

- Do they talk with you about real topics that matter to you or do they stay with the surface-level?

- Do you feel like they have enough emotional intelligence to hold a real conversation?

---

4. Are They Your Cheerleader?

Okay, this one's important. You want someone who *celebrates* your wins, big and small. Whether you just landed a promotion or successfully folded your laundry the same day it came out of the dryer (miraculous, right?), they should be the first ones cheering you on.

Checklist Question:

- Who's hyping you up like you're Beyoncé headlining Coachella?

- Do they brag about how amazing you are to their friends and family?

- Do they support your friends and family when they have something going on?
- Who's the first person you want to call when something awesome happens or even when something mildly interesting happens?

---

5. Do They Challenge You (in a Fun Way)?

No one needs a partner who's a total pushover. You want someone who challenges you—and keeps things exciting but doesn't turn every conversation into a competition. If they push you to grow and manage to do it without making you feel like you're in a constant performance review, that's gold.

Checklist Question:

- Who challenges you in ways that make you better (not just pushing you to do things they like, such as skydiving or eating food you don't like)?
- Do they hold you accountable when you say you are going to do something and you don't?
- Do they hold themselves accountable when they say they are going to do something and they don't?
- Who makes you want to be the best version of yourself, but not because they're judging your every move?

---

6. Do Your Values Line Up?

Let's be real—if your idea of "spontaneous fun" is organizing your bookshelf, and their idea is disappearing off the grid for a week without warning, we might have a problem. You don't need to be identical, but if your core values are way off, it's only going to get more awkward from here.

Checklist Question:

- Who aligns with your values on the big stuff, like family, work, and whether or not pineapple belongs on pizza?

- Which one would you say would get more answers right about you on a dating show game?

- Which of these people would you like to sit next to your grandmother for an hour while you are helping with other tasks?

- Who do you picture sharing those values with in ten years? (Because trust me, "opposites attract" isn't always the fairytale you think it is.)

---

7. Gut Feeling (a.k.a. Listen to Your Intuition, Dummy)

Your gut is smarter than you think. If one person makes your heart flutter while the other gives you that weird, unsettled feeling, guess what? Your gut is trying to tell you something. This isn't rocket science. Trust yourself because your gut already knows what's up.

Checklist Question:

- Who's the one that just feels *right*? (Come on, you know who.)

- Which one gives you goosebumps, butterflies, or fanny flutters (Shout out to my Brits for that lovely saying)?

- Which one would you rather have spent the night more than once a week?

- Which person do you genuinely *want* to text back (and not just because you're bored)?

---

8. *Who Do You See in Your Real Life?*

This is where the rubber meets the road. Who can you imagine being part of your actual, day-to-day life? It's great that they're fun on a Saturday night, but what about Tuesday morning when you're half-awake and grumbling over coffee? Do they fit into your real world, or are they just fun to look at from a distance?

Checklist Question:

- Who do you see blending into your life like they've always been there?

- You get a free trip to Iceland. You can only take one of these two (or 6, no judgement here) people. Who is coming?

- Who would you get a dog with? (This is a real commitment, people!)

- Who can you picture hanging out with your friends, meeting your family, or dealing with your ridiculous work schedule without running for the hills?

The Final Verdict: Who's Worth the Rose?

Once you've gone through this checklist, it's time to stop overthinking. Let's face it: you probably already know who's in the lead. Sometimes, it's just a matter of putting it all in perspective. Who's the person you'd be sad to let go of? Who makes you feel like you're on top of the world (without making you dizzy)? It's not about picking "the perfect person"—it's about picking the one who feels perfect *for you*.

So go ahead, make the choice. And if you need to sleep on it… well, maybe a few more dates wouldn't hurt.

Story Time: When Making Your Choice Backfires

Picture this: I am twenty and deep in the dating chaos, juggling five people like I've got romantic Cirque du Soleil ambitions and flexibility. Among them are two guys, let's call them, Phil— who also both happen to be my coworkers at the gym on campus because, of course, my life is a sitcom. Phil #1, seeing my indecision, calmly drops an ultimatum: either we get serious, or he's out. The nerve! Yet also, somehow, hot and the call to action I probably needed.

Not wanting to trust my caffeinated, overworked brain, I enlisted my best friend—a connoisseur of cheap wine and questionable judgment. Together, we spread out on my living room floor with sticky notes, pens, and the Pinot Noir equivalent of rocket fuel.

Time for a pros-and-cons list on Phil #1. Pros: hilarious, driven, social, and can keep up with me in an intellectual debate and, uh, other "extracurricular activities." Cons: basically, it was just the ultimatum, which I realized might not be so bad—at least he had standards. After a few sips of liquid courage, I decided Phil #1 was the one to focus on. I mean, I had to pick someone eventually, right?

So, I craft a series of heartfelt breakup texts for the other four, including Phil #2. Something empathetic yet firm, offering a phone call or even an in-person chat if they needed "closure." (Ah, twenty-year-old me, so earnest, so naïve.) Then I write the "We're going all-in!" text for Phil #1, telling him I can't stop thinking about him and need to see him tonight.

Cue disaster: I mixed up the messages. Phil #2 receives the green light, you're so special text instead of the break-up note, while Phil #1 gets the breakup text. Like an overconfident trapeze artist, I slip and fall spectacularly.

Unaware of my blunder, I invite Phil #2 to meet me at my gym to "celebrate." He shows up, grinning like a lottery winner, holding a fistful of condoms, eager to use every one of them. I was completely mortified when I realized I was going to have to do this awkward conversation in person and let him know that the sexy message he got was actually meant for another Phil. It went over about as well as J.D. Vance at a Drag Brunch fundraiser for Planned Parenthood.

Then I raced to Phil #1's place to explain that I'm not a full-time chaos agent, just part-time. It takes some groveling, a few more apologies than I'd planned, and maybe a dash of my unrelenting charm. Eventually, Phil #1 is convinced I'm just delightfully clumsy with my romantic communication, not maliciously confused.

Moral of the story: Label your Phils, double-check your texts, and never underestimate the power of a good pros-and-cons list. When in doubt, choose a partner who'll understand that sometimes your love life could use a personal assistant.

Chapter 16
Success Stories: They Exist, Apparently

Believe it or not, amidst the endless swiping, ghosting, and regrettable matches, some people actually manage to find love online. I know—it sounds like a myth, like Bigfoot or a well-organized sock drawer, but I'm here to tell you it *does* happen. There are real, live human beings out there who swiped right on someone and are now blissfully posting couple selfies and tagging each other in sappy social media posts. I mean, it's annoying, but it's also kind of sweet.

So, what are the odds? Honestly, they're slim. But sometimes, just when you're about to delete the app and swear off dating forever, you meet someone who makes you think, "Okay, maybe this can work." And before you know it, you're *that* couple—the ones at dinner parties casually saying, "We met on a dating app!" like it's some sort of fairy tale.

The Unicorn Couple

We all know one. The couple that makes you think, "How on earth did *they* manage to find each other online?" They seem so perfectly matched; it's like the dating gods themselves swiped right for them. They've got the shared hobbies, the cute couple photos, and an inside joke about how they almost swiped left on each other but didn't because *fate* intervened (or because the other person's dog was cute enough to make them reconsider).

The unicorn couple is proof that online dating *can* work, but they're also a walking reminder of how rare that success story is. They'll smile and tell you how they knew right away that they were meant to be while you sit there, wondering if you're ever going to find someone who can make it past the second date without vanishing into thin air.

Story Time: How I Met Shawn

Let me tell you about my unicorn story because I never thought I'd be one of those people who met someone special on a dating app. Shawn and I swiped right on Bumble, but neither was looking for love. In fact, we were both very much *not* looking for anything serious. We'd been burned by love before, and the idea of jumping into something meaningful wasn't exactly at the top of our to-do lists. We both just wanted casual, no-strings-attached engagements.

But then we met.

From the very beginning, there was something different about our connection. I don't know if it was the easy conversation or the fact that we both had zero expectations, but that first date was nothing like the ones I'd had before. Let me set the scene. I had just broken up with my partner of three years, who I was still living with, because we had bought a house together, and I was looking for a new place.

 I know! I was that person.

I was on my Rumspringa, and man, was I killing it.

At the time, I had eight partners, and to be honest, I wasn't that excited about this date. Do not get me wrong, Shawn was sexy, funny, and kind, and he had a great head on his shoulders. We had some good banter, but I really did not have the bandwidth to take on another person.

I was on my way to the date when I got a call from a friend who was having a particularly shitty day, and she asked if I could meet her for a drink. I let her know I had a date, but she sounded like she could use someone to talk to, so I texted Shawn and said, "How much do you like me?" Now, if you know me, you know that I say this in a tone like a kid who is about to ask you for a favor, and I am doing it with the biggest puppy dog eyes you have ever seen because I do expect to get my way.

But let us remember that Shawn does not know me, and this is in a text message, so I saw the three dots come on screen and disappear about four times before he wrote something to the effect of "Oh wow, okay, so... um, I know we haven't met yet, but I'd say you are cool and I have enjoyed getting to know you! I think we've got a lot in common, and I'm genuinely excited to meet you and see if we click as much in real life as we do over text. So yeah, I guess I like you... but in a totally normal, not weird, I-promise-I'm-not-a-creep way, lol."

Oh, Jesus... I completely blundered this date before it even got started. I made the mistake of using a phrase that only those close to me would understand, and he probably thought I was a crazy person. I almost crashed my car trying to call him to explain that I was not trying to ascertain how into me he was but more wanting to know if I could push back our date 20 minutes so I could chat with a friend. I called him, and he answered on the first ring and casually said, "Hey, you."

I know this is a weird thing, but I thought his answer on the first ring was an instant red flag. I am constantly an over- or under-red flagger. I either think the weirdest things are red flags, like answering on the first ring, or that having 4 baby daddies, no job, and face tattoos are just pink flags, not red ones. I know, I know, I am working on it in therapy. That will be the title of my 9th book, "My Therapist Says They're Red Flags, I Say They're Challenges."

Also, he was literally just texting me, so of course, he was going to answer in the first ring.

Anyways... I digress. The conversation went something like this:

Me:

"Hey Shawn, I swear I am not a weirdo; okay, that's not true; I am, but I was not really asking you if you liked me. I was really trying to do this cutesy thing I do when I need a favor. Is it okay if we push our date back by 20 minutes? A friend of mine really needs my help with something, but I promise I am worth the wait! Also, I will have to leave by 7 because I have a witches' party to get to.

Side note: I have this unbelievably talented, gorgeous, badass friend who throws a witch's party every year. We eat under a full moon, have delicious drinks next to a fire with blue flames, do tarot card readings, sacrifice a person who votes for anti-trans legislation, you know... the usual.

Shawn:
20 minutes? Wow! Already pushing the boundaries, huh? I see how it is. The next thing I know, it'll be 30 minutes. You are lucky you are cute, Ms. Jackson."

Me:
Oh... only Ms. Jackson if your nasty.. I swear I'm not trying to stand you up! Just trying to keep my superhero status intact for my friends. I'll be there, cape and all. You just need to show up to the restaurant 20 minutes later.

Shawn:
Well, I guess I can let it slide this time. But only because you're saving the day. I'll be there, dramatically checking my watch every five minutes. No pressure.

Me:

Phew, glad you're so understanding. I'll make up for it, I promise. The first round's on me!

Shawn:

Now we're talking! Alright, 20 minutes. But I'm keeping track—I'll expect a full recap of your heroic deeds when you get here.

My friend arrived, and we chatted about what was going on in her life, and it was definitely going to be longer than 20 minutes. Right as I was getting ready to text Shawn, he walked in. My friend turns to me and says, "Oh, girl. You are welcome. That guy is a dork. There is no way it would work out." Now granted, he was in a button-up short-sleeve with astronauts on them. The man was not coming in an Armani suit. I thought it was adorable. Shawn walked up confidently and introduced himself, and you would have thought he was meeting us both for drinks like he had done hundreds of times before. It went a little something like this.

Shawn:

"So, this is where the trouble starts, huh?" (He nods at both of us smiling.) "I finally get to meet the famous friend who stole all my date time."

Me:

(laughing) "She is good at vetting my dates."

Friend:

(teasing) "I'm just doing my due diligence! Someone's gotta keep her safe. You know, protecting her from all the dads in NASA shirts."

Shawn:

(laughing nervously) "I mean, guilty as charged. Dad jokes are

kind of my thing. But hey, if you're the gatekeeper to more of her time, I better be on my best behavior, huh?"

Friend:

(mock serious) "Exactly. So, what's your best dad joke? Impress me."

Shawn:

(pretending to think hard) "Hmm, alright, here goes: What did the ocean say to the beach? Nothing, it just waved. *(He grins, clearly pleased with himself.)*

Me:

(groaning and laughing) "Oh no, you actually went for it!"

Friend:

(sarcastically clapping) "Okay, okay, points for confidence. I see why she likes you. Brave enough to drop a dad joke on the first meet-up."

Shawn:

(grinning) "It's my secret weapon. That, and apparently, making a date fit into 30 minutes since you all are headed to a witch's party.

Me:

(playfully) "Hey! It was a *very* important gathering, thank you. We will be casting spells... or, you know, just drinking cocktails in black hats."

Shawn:

(laughing) "Ah, see? Now I understand why you're both so powerful. Witches' cocktails, that explains everything." *(He glances at my friend)* "So, are you the coven leader, or just the second in command?"

Friend:
(with a wink) "Oh, I'm definitely the leader."

Me:
(laughing) "This is why I brought her along, just to scare you off before the date even started."

Shawn:
(smiling, clearly charmed) "Well, too late for that. If surviving this witch's council is the price to pay for spending more time with you, I'll take my chances."

My friend left us to our date, and there was no awkward small talk, no pretense. We were just ourselves. This was the first date in years where I actually felt nervous. I have been on many dates, and I always had the confidence to know that if it did not work out, it was not a big deal because there were always others out there. This guy, though, there was something different. My heart was racing; I found myself getting red as he made me laugh. Was I blushing? The woman who did not blush. What was happening?

We sat there, talking for only 20 minutes because our date got cut entirely too short, and the more we talked, the more I realized that I really didn't want it to end. As we split the check, I realized this wasn't going to be just a casual fling. It felt different. He felt different. He walked me to my car, and I was expecting a kiss. I am not ashamed to tell you that about 90% of my first dates at this point either ended in 20 minutes because I wasn't feeling it or it ended with a steamy make-out session because, you know… Rumspringa.

So, when he looked at me with those soulful, sexy eyes and said, "Let's do this again but make it to 30 minutes," then gave me a warm hug that made me melt and told me to have a great time at my party, I got into my car, my breath caught, and I literally said, "Fuck. I am totally fucked." I knew from those 20 minutes that my life was about to change in a big way. I wasn't quite prepared for how, but I knew it would. From the minute that man moonwalked into my life, I knew I would never be the same.

So yeah, I'm one of those people now—the ones who tell their friends, "We met on Bumble!" with a little smirk because no one expects that to be the beginning of a love story.

The Secret Ingredient: Luck (and Maybe a Little Magic)

Here's the unvarnished truth about online dating success stories: the secret ingredient isn't your perfectly curated profile, your witty one-liners, or even those flawless selfies taken in perfect lighting. Those things are helpful of course—I mean I wrote literal chapters on them—but really, it's about plain old luck. The kind that can feel as elusive as finding a billionaire like Elon Musk's humility or sense of decency.

No one wants to admit it, but so much of online dating comes down to being in the right place at the right time—swiping right just as they do the same, the stars aligning in that tiny window between deleting the app in frustration and re-downloading it in a moment of weakness.

You might match with someone amazing on your very first day, feeling like the universe is giving you a high-five. Or you might find yourself swiping through 500 profiles, each one blurring into the next, before you stumble upon someone who can hold a conversation that doesn't make you want to "accidentally" drop your phone from a 30-story building.

It's a numbers game, sure, but it's also a twisted game of timing and a sprinkle of fate. Think about it: you're sifting through a digital sea of potential matches, all while they're doing the same, both of you are hoping to catch a glimpse of something—or someone—that makes you pause. It's like trying to find a needle in a haystack while being blindfolded, and the haystack is on fire.

Let's face it: you can have the most stellar profile with photos that would make a supermodel jealous and a bio that's the perfect blend of humor and depth. But if Lady Luck isn't on your side, you might as well be shouting into the void until you lose your voice. And don't even get me started on algorithms—those mysterious forces that seem to think your perfect match is a picture of a person's back facing a waterfall or someone whose entire bio reads as a negative Yelp review on dating.

But here's the kicker: when luck does strike, it feels like pure magic. All those endless swipes and awkward first messages suddenly become worth it when you connect with someone who gets your obscure movie references and laughs at your terrible puns. It's in those moments you realize that maybe, just maybe, the dating app gods have smiled upon you.

So what's the takeaway here? Keep swiping and hoping, and maybe carry a lucky charm. Because in the wild world of online dating, sometimes all you need is a little bit of luck—and perhaps a glass of wine or a favorite snack—to keep you going. After all, you never know when you might just hit the jackpot.

Chapter 17

Red Flags and Rainbows—What to Watch For in Your New Relationship

You've made it past the talking stage, the endless back-and-forth texting, and you've even survived the first few dates without running for the hills. Now, you've gone and made it *exclusive*. Cue the fireworks! You're officially in that exciting—and slightly nerve-wracking—phase where you're figuring out whether your connection is built to last or just a good fling with an expiration date.

But hold up. Just because you've locked things down doesn't mean you can start ignoring those little red flags that might start waving in the background. They're subtle, they're sneaky, but they're there. And I am here to help you spot them before you end up knee-deep in relationship drama, wondering why you didn't notice them sooner.

Here's your guide to red flags that could be lurking behind all those cute selfies and sweet messages. Don't worry; I have also included a few green flags because not *everything* is a red flag (promise!).

Red Flag #1: They're Suddenly Super Clingy

It's cute when someone wants to spend time with you. What's not cute? When they can't seem to function without constant validation, or they freak out if you don't text back within 2.5 minutes.

Checklist Questions:

- Do they get weirdly possessive when you hang out with friends or mention plans without them?
- Do they not have friends or interests of their own?
- Have they texted you "I miss you" after you just left them 45 minutes ago?
- Are they constantly checking up on your social media activity? (If you can't post a picture of your brunch without getting a "Where are you?" text… yeah, that's a flag.)

Pro Tip: It's great that they like you—but you're not their emotional support animal. If they're suffocating you now, it's probably not going to get better. Set boundaries and see how they respond. If they panic, that's your cue.

Red Flag #2: They Avoid Tough Conversations Like It's Their Job

You bring up a sensitive topic, and suddenly, they're "too busy" or "not in the mood to talk about this right now." Newsflash: emotional avoidance doesn't disappear once you're exclusive.

Checklist Questions:

- Have they dodged every attempt to talk about serious stuff like future plans, emotional baggage, or how they feel about pineapple on pizza?
- Do they suddenly turn into ghosts whenever you try to define relationship goals, finances, or, meeting their family?

- It is their solution to problems: "Let's just talk about it later."

Pro Tip: Relationships are built on communication, not avoidance. If they're consistently dodging real conversations, you might want to think twice before investing your emotional energy.

Red Flag #3: Everything Is Always Someone Else's Fault

Ah, the classic "blame game." If your new partner never seems to be at fault for anything in their life, it's time to dig deeper. They've been late to every date because of traffic? Every ex is *totally* crazy? Spoiler: it's probably not always that the universe is conspiring against them.

Checklist Questions:

- Do they constantly play the victim? ("I only acted like that because my boss is such a jerk!")
- Is it always someone else's fault when plans go wrong? (*"The GPS lied to me!"*)
- Have they called their ex crazy… multiple times?

Pro Tip: If they can't take responsibility for anything now, good luck navigating the inevitable challenges that come with a long-term relationship. Accountability isn't just a buzzword—it's essential.

Red Flag #4: They're Hot and Cold—And Not in a Cute Katy Perry Way

One minute, they're super sweet; the next, they're distant. This push-pull dynamic can be confusing and exhausting. Relationships should make you feel secure, not like you're on an emotional rollercoaster.

Checklist Questions:

- Are they super affectionate one day and then distant the next?
- Do they send mixed signals about where the relationship is going?
- Are you constantly left wondering if they're really into this or just kind of... there?

Pro Tip: Stability is sexy. If they keep you guessing all the time, it might be time to have a real talk about what they actually want. And if they can't give you a clear answer? That's your answer.

Red Flag #5: You're Getting the Family Runaround

Family doesn't have to be involved immediately, but if you've been exclusive for a while and they're still acting like introducing you to their family is the equivalent of launching a space mission, take note.

Checklist Questions:

- Have they kept you at arm's length from their family or friends with no real explanation?

- Are they super secretive about where they spend the holidays or important events?
- Does their family only seem to exist in vague, passing mentions?

Pro Tip: If they're serious about you, they'll eventually want to introduce you to their world. If you're months into a relationship and you've never met a single person in their life, it's worth asking why.

Red Flag #6: You're Always Walking on Eggshells

You shouldn't feel like you're navigating a minefield every time you bring up something that's bothering you. If you're afraid to express your feelings because you don't know how they'll react—major red flag.

Checklist Questions:

- Do you hesitate to bring up issues because you're afraid of how they'll react?
- Have they ever snapped or overreacted when you brought up something minor?
- Does every disagreement feel like walking into a storm?

Pro Tip: Disagreements are normal, but if you're afraid to have them, that's a problem. Healthy communication means addressing issues without fear of a blow-up. You deserve to feel heard, not silenced.

Green Flags to Look For (Because Not Everything Is a Disaster)

But hey, it's not all doom and gloom. If you've made it this far and you're seeing *none* of these red flags, you might just have a keeper. Here are some green flags to be on the lookout for:

Green Flag #1: They're Consistent

No wild mood swings or confusing behavior. They're steady, and you always know where you stand with them. You know, when they tell you that they will be there, they will.

Green Flag #2: They Encourage Your Growth

They want you to be your best self and actively encourage your goals, passions, and growth. If they're your biggest cheerleader, you're in the right place.

Green Flag #3: They're Open to Tough Conversations

If they're willing to dive into the messy, uncomfortable topics without shutting down, that's a huge green flag. It means they're in this for the long haul and aren't afraid of real commitment.

Final Thoughts: Trust Yourself and Keep Your Eyes Open

At the end of the day, red flags don't always mean immediate doom, but they're signs to pay attention to. Trust your gut, communicate clearly, and remember you deserve someone who makes you feel safe, appreciated, and supported—not someone who leaves you questioning everything.

Now, go forth and enjoy the exclusive relationship ride—just keep an eye on the flags along the way!

Chapter 18

How to Sabotage Your New Relationship Before It Even Starts (And How to Stop)

Now, let's not pretend that all red flags are one-sided. We all carry some baggage, and we all have our own set of flags, and not all of them are green. Ah, the early days of a new relationship—when everything is sparkly, and you're eagerly swiping through your camera roll for the perfect photo to send because you want to impress them but also not look like you are trying too hard. You're cautiously optimistic, maybe even *hopeful*, that this could be "the one," but then your brain gets in the way, and things start to go south *real* fast.

Yep, we've all been there. Welcome to the self-sabotage zone, where your thoughts spiral, overthinking kicks into high gear, and suddenly, you're turning a perfectly good relationship into a Netflix series called *How to Ruin Everything in 10 Days*. But don't worry, it doesn't have to be that way! Here's a guide to some of the classic self-sabotaging we all fall into—and how to avoid tripping over them before it's too late.

---

1. Overanalyzing Every. Single. Thing.

They sent a smiley face but no heart emoji. What does it mean?!

If there were an Olympic event for overthinking, you'd probably be wearing gold like Simone Biles. Shout out to that GOAT. The early stages of a relationship are fertile grounds for letting your mind run wild—because nothing says romance like questioning every text, analyzing every emoji, and reading between lines that don't even exist.

How You're Sabotaging: Overanalyzing can make you paranoid and self-conscious, creating problems that don't actually exist. By constantly wondering what *everything* means, you forget to enjoy the relationship.

How to Stop: Take a deep breath. Not every text needs to be decoded like you're breaking into the Pentagon or trying to figure out what the fuck Trump's tweets mean. If something's bothering you, ask directly instead of spiraling into your own mental abyss. Clarity is your best friend.

---

2. Moving Too Fast (Emotionally or Otherwise)

You've been on a few dates, and things are going great. Naturally, you've already started thinking about how beautiful their last name is, picked out a future dog, and mentally chosen a wedding venue. Slow down, Sha'Carri Richardson—this is dating, not the 100-meter dash.

How You're Sabotaging: When you rush into things emotionally, you risk freaking the other person out or skipping important stages in getting to know each other. No one wants to feel like they're suddenly starring in 90-Day Fiancée because that shit is legit crazy.

How to Stop: Relationships are like fine wine; they need time to breathe. Focus on enjoying the present without racing to the finish line. Let things develop naturally instead of mentally fast-forwarding to "happily ever after."

3. Not Being Your Authentic Self

It's tempting to show off only the shiny, impressive parts of yourself in the beginning—after all, you want to impress them. But soon enough, you're pretending to like things you don't, laughing at jokes that aren't funny, or even holding back your real opinions just to keep things moving smoothly. Newsflash: this never ends well.

How You're Sabotaging: When you're not being authentic, the other person ends up falling for a version of you that doesn't actually exist. Eventually, the real you will show up, and it'll feel like a bait-and-switch. Plus, pretending is exhausting.

How to Stop: Let your real self shine through, quirks and all. If they don't vibe with the real you, it's better to find out now than later. Authenticity is attractive, and they'll appreciate the real you if they're worth your time.

---

4. Playing Games (We're Not in High School Anymore)

Remember the "wait three days to text back" rule? Or sending cryptic messages to seem mysterious? Yeah, it's time to toss out those outdated playbooks. Playing games might seem like a way to keep things interesting, but it usually ends in confusion, frustration, or someone giving up entirely.

How You're Sabotaging: Playing hard to get, sending mixed signals, or being intentionally distant can leave the other person feeling unsure about your intentions. Plus, it's exhausting trying to keep up the "mystery" when all you want is to send a text like a normal human being.

How to Stop: Be direct. If you like them, show it. If you want to text them, do it. You're both adults (presumably), so there's no need for childish games.

---

5. *Getting Stuck in "Comparison Mode"*

You're having a good time, but you can't help but think about your ex—or that one time your best friend had a similar situation. Or, worse, you're scrolling through social media, comparing your fledgling romance to everyone else's highlight reels.

How You're Sabotaging: Comparing your current relationship to past ones or other people can suck the joy out of what you have. Every relationship is different, and no "right" timeline or formula exists. Constantly comparing will make you feel like you're missing something—even if you're not.

How to Stop: Focus on your own relationship. It's fine to reflect on what worked (or didn't) in the past but don't let that cloud the potential of what you have now. And for the love of everything, stop comparing your relationship to social media—it's not real life.

---

6. *Assuming the Worst*

They didn't text you back for a few hours, and now you're convinced they've lost interest, found someone else, or are planning to ghost you. Your brain is on a rollercoaster of worst-case scenarios, and suddenly, a perfectly fine relationship is now a horror show in your head.

How You're Sabotaging: Assuming the worst about every little thing creates anxiety and tension that wouldn't otherwise exist.

You're jumping to conclusions without giving the other person a chance to explain or simply... live their life.

How to Stop: Chill. Give them the benefit of the doubt. People have lives, and just because they didn't respond immediately doesn't mean they're plotting your emotional demise. If there's a real issue, they'll let you know—or you can ask.

---

7. *Trying to Be Perfect*

In the early stages of a relationship, it's easy to fall into the trap of trying to be "perfect"—saying the right things, never making mistakes, and generally acting like some idealized version of yourself. But newsflash: nobody's perfect. And honestly? Trying to be is the fastest way to make things fall apart.

How You're Sabotaging: Trying to be perfect means you're not being authentic. It's pressuring both people in the relationship as they must live up to unrealistic expectations. Plus, perfection is boring. It's our quirks and flaws that make us interesting!

How to Stop: Embrace the messiness. It's okay to make mistakes, say the wrong thing, or have a bad day. The right person will appreciate you, your imperfections, and everything else. Remember, perfection is overrated.

Story Time: The Time When My Sabotage Backfired

Shawn and I went from 0 to 100 quickly. We had our second date uninterrupted this time. Shawn picked minigolf, and we tried to eat afterward, but everywhere was closed, so we drank our dinner and ended up making out for hours in my kitchen. After that, we were pretty much inseparable. We were both not quite ready to say we were exclusive, but we were spending a lot of time together at this point.

We were nestled on my overly plush couch, half a bottle of wine deep and just the right amount of tipsy. You know that sweet spot where your cheeks are warm, everything is a tad funnier, and your internal filter decides to take a smoke break. The soft glow of my pumpkin spice candle (Yes, I am THAT white girl... I really wish I wasn't, but alas...) bathed the room in a cozy light, and some Maggie Rogers was providing the perfect background music (If you do not know her, get your ass to Spotify. She has the voice of an angel). In that moment, glass halfway to my lips, I thought, *Oh no, I like him. Like, a lot.*

At this point, Shawn and I had been seeing each other for a few months. We were still dating other people—it was casual, no labels, just two people enjoying each other's company. But lately, things had started to feel different. The easy laughter, the way his hand found mine without thinking, the comfortable silences that didn't need filling—it all hinted at something more. And that terrified me.

You see, I had baggage. Major baggage. Like Real Housewives of whatever county packing for the Hamptons baggage. I was fresh out of a relationship that had left me feeling rejected and judged like I was somehow too much and not enough all at once. My ex had made me feel ashamed of who I was and what I wanted, leading me on for over three years without any intention of a real future. We'd moved in together, renovated a house, and I'd even reshaped my social life to fit his mold of "wife material." Spoiler alert: it didn't work out.

So here I was, cozying up to Shawn—a man who ticked all the boxes—and instead of leaning into it, my fight-or-flight response was screaming, "ABORT!" I was terrified of recommitting, being vulnerable, and opening up just to be let down again. Naturally, I did what any self-respecting, emotionally guarded person would do: I decided it was time to self-sabotage.

Fun Rocci fact: I am *exceptionally* good at self-sabotage. Olympic level. If there were medals for it, I'd have the equivalent of the 1904 United States team (239 of them, great trivia fact, you are welcome).

So, there we were, the air was thick with unspoken feelings, and I thought, *It's now or never. Time to scare him off before things get too real.* I turned to him, tucking a stray hair behind my ear—a nervous habit—and said, "You know, there's something I should probably tell you."

He looked at me with those stupidly sweet, calm eyes that seemed to see right through my bravado. "Alright," he said softly, "I'm listening."

I took a deep breath, feeling my heartbeat in my ears. "I, uh... I've been thinking a lot about what I want and feel I should be upfront." I paused for dramatic effect—or maybe to gather the courage to jump off this 1,000-foot cliff. "I've always wanted to be in a non-monogamous relationship."

I looked at his face closely, searching for any sign of recoil. When none came, I decided to up the ante. "And, also, I'm pansexual. So, you know... that's a thing."

For those not in the know—looking at you, dear Boomers—pansexuality means being attracted to people regardless of their gender identity. (Yes, Bob from the Yacht Club, that's a thing. Welcome to the 21st century.)

I braced myself, fully expecting him to do the polite nod followed by a swift exit or some vague excuse about an early morning. My ex had made me feel so much shame about who I was that I just assumed everyone would react like that. Internally, I was already drafting text messages to my friends about how "men are trash" and asking who would want to go out that weekend to let off some steam with me and "Balboa" because she would want to rage.

Shawn just blinked, his expression thoughtful. "Okay," he said simply. "And?"

I blinked back. "And?" I parroted, momentarily thrown off my game.

"Yeah, and?" he repeated, a small smile tugging at the corners of his mouth.

I stared at him, confusion mixing with the Pinot Noir swirling in my system. "So... you're okay with that?" I asked, waiting for the catch.

He chuckled softly, reaching over to gently take my hand. "Rocci, I like you for who you are—all of you. I didn't sign up for some edited or watered-down version of you. Non-monogamous, pansexual—you could tell me you moonlight as a superhero, and I'd ask how I can support your crime-fighting career. You are bold, beautiful, intelligent, and so giving to those around you. I am honored to be in your life in any way, and I want to bask in your light, not dim it."

I felt a blush creep up my neck, and my eyes started to water. I literally had to look away from him and up at the ceiling. What was happening? I was not in control. This was not how this was supposed to go. "Are you sure? Because I'm kind of a lot. I mean, I come with a warning label and possibly a user manual."

He grinned, in that infuriatingly charming way he does that simultaneously melted my defenses and annoyed me. "Too late for warnings. Besides, I've always been good at reading between the lines."

I narrowed my eyes playfully. "You do realize I'm trying to sabotage this, right? You're not making it easy."

He laughed heartily. "Oh, I noticed. But unfortunately for you, I don't scare off easy."

I threw my hands up in mock exasperation. "Great. Just great. Here I am, giving you all the reasons you should need for an easy out, and you want to stay?"

He shrugged casually. "Look, I've got my own baggage. I was in a seventeen-year relationship—that's like a lifetime in celebrity marriages. I'm not looking for perfect; I'm looking for real. And you, my dear, are as real as it gets."

I couldn't help but smile at that. "Well, when you put it that way..."

He squeezed my hand gently. "Plus, I've always found 'a lot' to be way more interesting than 'not enough.' Keeps things exciting."

I shook my head, a laugh escaping my lips. "You realize this means you're stuck with me, right? No take-backs."

He leaned in closer, his eyes meeting mine and said "Wouldn't have it any other way."

And just like that, my grand plan to push him away blew up in my face. Instead of creating distance, I'd inadvertently pulled us closer together. It was both terrifying and exhilarating.

"Fine," I said with a faux sigh. "But don't say I didn't warn you."

He raised his glass, eyes twinkling. "To being a lot."

I clinked my glass against his. "Cheers to that."

As we settled back into the couch, the conversation flowed effortlessly, touching on everything from our favorite childhood cartoons to our most embarrassing moments. There was a warmth between us that I hadn't felt ever—a comforting certainty that maybe, just maybe, I didn't have to sabotage this.

It turns out that when someone accepts you for who you are, self-sabotage loses its appeal. Who knew? Lesson learned: Sometimes, the right person won't run away when you show them your scars; they'll trace them gently and remind you that they make you who you are.

Chapter 19
Surviving the Honeymoon: How to Keep the Spark Beyond Month Three

If you've made it this far in the book, you're armed with more than just snappy openers and a keen eye for red flags—you've also navigated the digital dating circus enough to find someone worth seeing beyond that glorious first month. Cue the confetti and pop that Champagne! Did you know that research says that new relationships are most at risk for dissolving in between 3-6 months? I am not a scientist, but I would venture to guess that is because this period often brings doubts like, "Did I make the right choice with this person? Did I settle? Is there something better out there?" On the flip side, some of us may find ourselves picking out the song for our first dance at our wedding.

We want something meaningful and easy, so how do you turn early chemistry into something that outlasts the honeymoon phase? Let's tie everything we've talked about—boundaries, red flags, question-of-the-day magic, and owning your weirdness—into a guide for sustaining those giddy "Is this real?" vibes well past the dreaded three-to-six-month slump.

---

1. Remember the Red Flags—Yours and Theirs

We've spent an entire chapter on recognizing and managing red flags, so don't abandon that knowledge now that you're "official." Every quirk, boundary, and communication style matters—whether it's chronic over-planning or borderline-inappropriate sarcasm. The same goes for your partner's strong tendencies or borderline habits: ignoring them at month four leads to shock at month seven when those traits inevitably resurface.

Tie-In: If your biggest red flag is hyper-independence—like disappearing on your partner for days without warning—apply what you've learned about setting expectations. And if your partner has shown questionable behaviors—like ghosting friends whenever they're in a relationship—keep that on your radar as you move forward.

---

2. Balance Fun with Foundations

Remember how, in previous chapters, we tackled the pitfalls of being too serious or too casual? Early on, it's easy to get stuck in the "everything's perfect" mode or obsess over long-term compatibility from day one. The key is finding a balance. Flirt, tease, plan spontaneous outings (like that random trapeze class you read about), *and* have genuine conversations about finances, family, or future goals—just not every night.

Example: Feel free to do that silly "question of the day" activity we discussed—like "Which movie universe would you live in?"—while also finding time to talk about whether you both believe in renting vs. buying a place in the future. It's like combining dessert and veggies on one plate—there's room for both, and they are equally important.

---

3. Keep Up Your Boundaries and Routines

We hammered boundaries into your head for a reason: not setting them is the fastest way to lose yourself in a new romance. If you were actively working on your own red flags—like a habit of overcommitting—don't abandon that progress. In fact, hold firm to the healthy patterns you established:

- Weekly "me time" for that pottery class or gaming session with friends.

- Check-ins on your schedule so neither of you feel blindsided when you're slammed at work.

Tie-In: This is where the "scheduling check-ins" from the messaging and boundaries chapters come into play. Let them know if you can't do dinners daily because you're focusing on your passion project. Transparency beats simmering resentment every time.

---

4. Ask Weird Questions Even After You're "Official"

It's tempting to slip into the bland "How was your day?" routine once you've moved from dating to "I guess we're seeing each other a lot." Resist the urge. Keep up the quirky questions that made the initial texting phase so fun. It's a simple, lighthearted way to keep learning about each other.

Example:

- "If our relationship was a board game, which would it be, and who's winning right now?"

- "What fictional couple do you think we're most like—and why?"

A little silliness keeps you both curious and engaged, reminding each other why you clicked in the first place.

5. Co-Adventures: Shared and Solo

We covered the importance of trying new things with your partner—like an escape room or a new food truck you discovered. But also, don't ditch your existing world. Balancing shared activities (so you create shared memories) and solo pursuits (so you maintain your individuality) is a constant dance.

Practical Tip: Schedule one "joint adventure" each month—maybe that weird axe-throwing bar or an up-and-coming indie band concert. And also, schedule a separate time for your own hobbies or friend groups so you aren't morphing into a two-headed creature that forgets how to function alone.

---

6. Regular Check-Ins (Not Just for Emergencies)

You learned from the meltdown stories in earlier chapters that failing to communicate is a surefire way to end up with accidental breakups, wrong-Phil fiascos, and turkey dog "philanthropy." To avoid these pitfalls, consider having a casual "relationship progress check" every month or so—it works wonders.

Example:

- "Hey, how are you feeling about how much time we spend together? You still good with my weekly board game night with the crew?"
- "Any big things on your mind we haven't chatted about?"

Cue a short, honest talk that can prevent big issues from snowballing.

7. Keep Your Quirk and Your Circle

Your friends, family, and personal flair are part of what made you interesting. If you start skipping friend gatherings or stop wearing your beloved tie-dye socks because your new partner finds them "meh," you risk losing the very spark that made them (and you) excited in the first place.

Tie-In: Remember how you recognized your own red flags? One might be "giving up personal style to please others." Nip that in the bud by proudly rocking those tie-dye socks and inviting your partner to admire or gently tease them—either way, you stay authentically you.

---

8. Beat the 'Grass Is Greener' Syndrome

Online dating can foster a fear-of-missing-out mentality. "What if there's someone *even better* out there?" Accept that curiosity is normal but doesn't have to sabotage a good thing. Remember the meltdown stories from earlier chapters: juggling multiple matches can get messy fast. If this person checks your major boxes, consider investing energy in building a lasting bond rather than chasing shiny new profiles.

Pro Tip: If you're feeling those "what if?" jitters, talk to your partner. Maybe you both want to keep it open for now or maybe you just need reassurance. Honesty (and references to your thoroughly researched "red flag" chapter) can stop anxiety before it grows.

9. Celebrate the Small Wins

Whether it's your partner remembering your big work presentation or you managing to nail dinner for two without burning the house down, celebrating little triumphs reaffirms why you two click. Don't wait for a birthday or major anniversary—send a silly "Congrats on not forgetting your lunch today" text or host a mini toast to the fact that your schedules aligned for a Friday movie night.

Tie-In: This echoes our earlier theme of "effort stands out." Just like Shawn's conference livestream move, small gestures add up and keep that honeymoon glow shining longer.

Final Words: The 6-Month Mark Is Yours to Win

Remember all those lessons from our earlier chapters—spotting red flags, owning your own quirks, checking your boundaries, and mastering top-notch messaging? They don't expire just because you've moved to "we're dating" status. In fact, now is when you apply them more than ever.

Be mindful of both passion and real talk. Keep your sense of individuality intact. Keep it fun, but don't dodge the deeper issues. Celebrate wins—big or small—and schedule honest conversations about what's working. If you balance all these elements, you'll find that making it past month three or six isn't luck—it's the natural result of a relationship built on understanding, humor, and genuine care.

So go forth, flirt with that puzzle date idea, ask your partner another offbeat question (like, "Which animal would you reincarnate as), and continue weaving that delightful tapestry of inside jokes, supportive gestures, and boundary-respecting conversations. By combining the best parts of the "I can't stop smiling" honeymoon phase with real compatibility checks, you're setting the stage for something truly worth turning off your dating apps for.

Story Time: The Becky Debacle (A Cautionary Tale)

Picture me—fresh off the heels of a seven-year relationship that went down in flames—feeling about as stable as a Jenga tower in the middle of an earthquake. Then along comes "Becky" (yes, a man with no hair and a traditionally feminine name), bringing all the worst traits of an insecure, macho narcissist. He arrived with sweet words and grand gestures, making me feel like I'd just won the Life Lottery after years of being undervalued. Let's just say I was *here* for it.

But buckle up because Becky turned out to be a jealous, insecure, cheating **twat waffle** who could teach a masterclass in emotional manipulation. He'd throw a fit about my male friends while conveniently forgetting to mention his own *female* friends sleeping over—then casually tell me the next day as if it were no big deal. When he accompanied me to social events, he'd schmooze everyone until they adored him... only to pick a fight with me right after so he could leave early and keep me chasing the fantasy he'd created. In other words, it was a nonstop rollercoaster of "Wait—*did that really happen?*"

As if emotional drama weren't enough, he also had me signing up for "adventures," which made zero sense for who I actually am. Let's talk about desert rock climbing in scorching heat that felt straight out of Mad Max: no newbie-friendly walls here—just a fiery wasteland that seemed personally offended by my existence.

I was terrified, but Becky insisted, "Live a little!" as if my instincts (and, I don't know, common sense) didn't matter.

Next, he dragged me to hours-long hot yoga in a remote yurt with no cell service—just me, Becky, and a sweaty chorus of strangers contorting our spines in 105-degree heat. Sure, I'm open to new experiences, but this was less "wellness" and more "extreme endurance test." Then came disc golf in a sketchy, graffiti-laden area that looked like it was waiting for a cameo in the next post-apocalyptic thriller. He'd grin and say, "Go get it, babe!" while I desperately scouted for exit routes in case a feral raccoon gang decided to show up.

I started ignoring my own interests—like weekly brunches and comedic open-mic nights (which bring me so much joy)—and basically morphed into a "Yes, Becky!" version of myself who barely recognized her own reflection. It was as if I'd handed him the keys to my identity, and honey, that is a highway to heartbreak.

But guess what? This *Goddess of the Universe* finally woke up. I remembered that my value, my passions, and my sense of self are **not** up for debate. No amount of flattery or "adventure" justifies losing who I am. And that's the moral of this story: when your gut whispers, "This is bananas," listen. If someone's "new experiences" feel more like a reality show you never auditioned for, it's time to change the channel.

You deserve someone who respects your boundaries, your interests, and your comfort level—someone who doesn't turn your social life into an emotional minefield or use flattery to mask deeply rooted insecurity. In short? Keep your feet planted firmly in your own identity because no sweet-talking narcissist should be allowed to rewrite your personal script.

So, here's to standing your ground, honoring your passions, and never letting anyone dull your shine. Trust me: losing yourself to please a toxic partner is one climb *no one* should ever attempt. Stay true to you, baby—and leave the desert drama for the movies.

Chapter 20

Sharing is Caring (Except When It's Not)—Navigating Ethical Non-Monogamy Without Losing Your Mind

So, here we are—ethical non-monogamy. The phrase alone is enough to make some people clutch their pearls and reach for their emergency Bible, but for me, it just makes sense. Yes, I know it's not for everyone; some folks hear "non-monogamy" and instantly think it's a code for "can't commit" or "perpetual cheater." But when you've spent your whole life never quite fitting into the "one person forever" box, you start to wonder, *Why am I forcing myself into this tiny, uncomfortable space?*

Spoiler alert: I'm done with the box and the societal expectations that come with it.

I've always been someone who's attracted to people for more than just their gender. I knew at about 13 that I was into women, but I grew up in a tiny community where the dating pool was more of a puddle, and the idea of being with a woman was as foreign as a good sushi bar in Kansas. Think conservative mountain town where the size of someone's truck defines their status in the community and is definitely indicative of their small dick energy—over*compensating much, Doug?*

For me, the attraction is about the whole package—personality, humor, intelligence, kindness—and sometimes, one package just doesn't fulfill every side of who I am. For a long time, I felt like the odd one out—even within the queer community. My attraction and fluidity never quite fit into one neat little label, and people tend to love labels. Especially my ex.

Let's call him *The Judge* because that's what he did—judge me like he was Simon Cowell and I was a tone-deaf contestant on *American Idol*. The minute I brought up ethical non-monogamy, it was like I'd suggested we join a cult or, worse, cancel football season. Suddenly, I was no longer the partner with different needs—I was a "whore" for even suggesting the idea.

I let my ex make me feel ashamed of who I was and what I wanted. I tried to squeeze myself into the tiny, suffocating life of a very vanilla, heterosexual relationship because I thought that's what I should do at 34—get married, have kids, settle down with someone "stable" who had a good job and a retirement plan. I convinced myself that this was the blueprint for happiness, but instead, I felt like I was slowly fading into the background of my own life. I'd never felt lower or more disconnected from who I really was.

But then I met Shawn, and suddenly everything changed. For the first time, I felt truly seen and supported. Shawn didn't just accept me—he celebrated the parts of me I had tried to hide. I've never felt more alive and authentic than I do with him.

Why Ethical Non-Monogamy?

It's not about chasing something *better*—it's about realizing that different parts of me crave different kinds of connections. Let's be real: expecting one person to tick every single box is like asking your toaster to also brew coffee. It's not a failure; it's just not realistic—despite what rom-coms like *Bridget Jones* might have made you believe.

But let me give you a reality check: ethical non-monogamy isn't some groovy, free-love utopia where everyone's dancing barefoot in a field, high-fiving over their emotional growth. It's not about secret hand signals or putting pineapples on your porch to signal you're "in the club." This is real life, and it comes with rules.

The rules? They're less about "anything goes" and more about boundaries, regular check-ins, and painfully honest communication. It's messy sometimes. It evolves constantly. What works for us might look completely different for someone else—and that's okay. This isn't a one-size-fits-all lifestyle; it's tailor-made, and for us, it fits just right.

Boundaries: The Glue That Keeps Us Together

When I first started exploring this with Shawn, I knew one thing: if this was going to work, we had to talk—a lot. You'd think two people who already get along well wouldn't need to check in so often, but ethical non-monogamy requires about ten times the communication of your average relationship. And lucky for him, I never shut up, so we're always having some sort of conversation about wants, desires, dates, and giving each other thoughts and advice on how to handle things.

Here's how we keep things running smoothly:

1. **Regular Check-Ins:** Whether we're sitting on the couch or grabbing a quick coffee, we always make time to ask, "How are you feeling about where we are in our relationship? Are you okay with that person I have a date with this week? Are you comfortable if I take it to the next level with them?" It sounds cheesy, like we're reciting lines from a self-help book, but it works. Emotional stuff can sneak up on you, and no one wants a surprise "I hate everything about this" moment.

2. **Transparency is Key:** No secrets, no sneaky rendezvous. We talk openly about who we're seeing and what those relationships look like. This is not some failed military "don't ask, don't tell" policy. It's more like, "I want to know how your date went because I care and because it helps me feel informed about where we are and what we're doing as a team."

3. **Respecting the Primary Relationship:** We're each other's anchors. No matter who else we're seeing, Shawn and I make it clear that we're each other's main event. That means prioritizing our relationship and making sure we feel secure and respected at all times. It's about making the relationship feel like a home base, not just a pit stop or something that gets attention after new dates.

4. **Boundaries, Boundaries, Boundaries:** Look, spontaneity is fun, but not when it comes to boundaries. We've drawn lines around what we're comfortable with, and we revisit those boundaries regularly to make sure everyone's happy. It's not a "set it and forget it" rotisserie chicken; relationships are fluid, and so are our needs.

The First Time Jealousy Hit—Like a Ton of Bricks

Now, let's get to the juicy part—the first time Shawn was intimate with someone else. I thought I was ready. Seriously, we talked about it endlessly. For context, dear reader, I've been in and out of the alternative lifestyle scene for about 10 years. This wasn't uncharted territory for me. But for Shawn? Total newbie. He never seemed jealous, so I assumed I'd be fine.

We set our boundaries, dissected our feelings, and I strutted into it feeling confident—maybe even a little smug. Look at me, all evolved and emotionally mature!

But then it happened. Shawn went on a date with this woman—let's call her *Yoga Girl* because, of course, she teaches yoga and has the flexibility of a Cirque du Soleil performer. This is not true, but you know your brain goes there when you start letting it go crazy. He was upfront about his plans, and I was all, "Have fun! Can't wait to hear about it!" Internally, I was giving myself a high-five for being the coolest girlfriend ever.

That day, I was spending time with my best friend, but my mind kept drifting. *What are they doing right now? Is she funnier than me? Can she touch her toes without groaning?* By the time he came home and called me to tell me about the date, I had spiraled into a jealous frenzy that would make Lisa 'Left Eye' Lopes look like Mother Teresa.

We have always had the rule that we tell each other every detail about the experience. So, as he began to recount every intimate moment, I was perched on the couch like a gargoyle, eyes narrow, spoon in hand like a weapon. "So, how was it?" I asked, trying to keep my voice casual but probably sounding like I was auditioning for a horror movie.

"It was good," he said cautiously. "We had a nice time." He could tell by my silence that I was struggling with the information that was shared.

"Rocci, what's really going on here?" he asked gently.

And that's when I lost it. "I don't want to share you!" I blurted out. "I thought I could handle it, but I can't! I want to be the only one!"

There it was—the ugly truth. Miss *I'm So Cool With Ethical Non-Monogamy* was actually a jealous mess.

Shawn took a deep breath. "It's okay to feel this way. I have felt upset and jealous too," he said softly. "But we need to talk about it."

I sat glaring at the phone. "Talk about what? That you had a great time with Miss Yoga Pants while I sat alone?"

I imagined him sitting with the phone in hand and trying to suppress a smile. "You told me to have fun."

"Well, I didn't mean it!" I exclaimed. "I was trying to be supportive, but I hate this! I hate that you're with someone else!"

He took a deep breath and shared. "Thank you for telling me how you feel," he said. "Let's figure this out together."

I sat looking at my phone, tears welling up. "I feel like a fraud. I wanted to be okay with this, but I'm not. I know that this is so selfish since you have had to be okay with me doing it. I am so sorry I am not stronger."

He told me that he wished he was there to hug me. "You're not a fraud. You're human. Feelings change, and that's okay. We can adjust our boundaries."

"Can we make a new rule that you're only allowed to date people who are less flexible than me?" I mumbled.

He chuckled. "Noted."

We spent the rest of the night talking—really talking. I admitted that I was jealous, that I felt insecure, and that the idea of him being with someone else made me want to set things on fire (figuratively, of course—no houses or shoes were harmed). He listened and validated my feelings, and together, we decided to take a step back and reevaluate what ethical non-monogamy looked like for us. I was able to work through my feelings and recognize that they were really coming from a fear of him being able to hold strong boundaries since this was such a new space for him, and I was afraid I might lose him. We were able to come to an understanding and I was reassured that night, and we were able to move forward stronger than before.

The Power of Communication (Again)

That experience taught me that even with all the preparation in the world, emotions can still catch you off guard. And that's okay. What's important is how you handle them. Instead of letting my jealousy fester or setting Shawn's clothes on fire in the bathtub (tempting as it was), we communicated.

We adjusted our boundaries:

- **No Overnight Stays**: At least for now, we agreed that overnights were off the table.

- **More Check-Ins:** We decided to have pre- and post-date discussions to gauge how we're both feeling.

- **Jealousy is Allowed:** We acknowledge that jealousy is a natural emotion and that it's okay to feel it. What's not okay is letting it dictate our actions without discussing it.

Why Ethical Non-Monogamy Works for Us (Most of the Time)

I've come to realize that ethical non-monogamy isn't about dodging commitment; it's about redefining what commitment can look like. For Shawn and I, it's trusting each other to explore connections with others while always remembering where home is. It's not a smooth, glossy fairy tale—it's messy, challenging, and sometimes downright awkward. But it's also real, and that's what matters.

I want to talk about that tired old saying, "They want their cake and to eat it too." Like, no kidding! What else are you supposed to do with cake? Frame it? Hurl it into traffic? Of course, I want to eat my cake—and while I'm at it, I'll take a slice of pie, some brownies, and a few éclairs. I want the whole damn bakery, and I'm not losing sleep over what anyone thinks about that.

But here's the thing—even in the best bakeries, sometimes you bite into something that doesn't sit quite right. That doesn't mean you close up shop. You tweak the recipe, make adjustments, and keep baking. Because, at the end of the day, it's all about creating something that works for you.

The Bottom Line

Ethical non-monogamy isn't a one-size-fits-all deal. It's complicated, requires a ridiculous amount of communication, and isn't without its challenges—like sudden bouts of Lisa 'Left Eye' Lopes-level jealousy. But for us, it's worth it. We've built a relationship that's flexible (pun intended), honest, and, most importantly, built on respect.

So here's to navigating love without losing your mind—or burning down any houses.

Chapter 21

Conclusion: Surviving the Dating Circus with a Grin (and a Few Memes)

And here we are—together at the end of this glorious, chaotic circus of modern romance. We've navigated seas of red flags, decoded hieroglyphic emoji bios, and even survived the dreaded seven-dates-in-one-day marathon (don't try that at home). We've met "sex gods" who required user manuals, non-monogamy mishaps that tested our nerves, and learned that sometimes "Let's take this to the next level" texts end up going to the wrong person. And let's not forget my mother's date with Discount Romeo at the circus, where Ed Hardy couture and turkey hot dog "philanthropy" combined for one of the most spectacularly misguided seduction attempts in recorded history.

If there's one big takeaway here, it's that the dating world is part comedy club, part funhouse—and you're simultaneously the headliner, the audience, and occasionally, the person mopping up spilled drinks. But fear not! You've got this. Armed with humor, self-awareness, and maybe an Idris Elba cocktail, you can stride into this big top with your head held high.

Let's sum it all up:

1. **Own Your Weirdness and Red Flags:**

    We've all got quirks—maybe you over-plan your life down to the minute, or you're emotionally constipated when it comes to being vulnerable. The key? Stop pretending you're a flawless Instagram influencer and start embracing your inner goofball. Acknowledge the red flags you bring to the table so you can manage them before they morph into a one-way ticket to Awkwardville.

2. **Boundaries, Boundaries, Boundaries:**

   Whether you're telling someone, "Yeah, no, I don't do 3 a.m. booty calls," or explaining that surprise trapeze lessons are not your idea of foreplay, clear communication, and firm boundaries keep everyone's expectations in check. No more code-speak or silent suffering. Life's too short to pretend you're into CrossFit when you'd rather be cross-stitching.

3. **Communication is King (or Queen, or Monarch of Your Choice):**

   Tell people what you want and what you definitely don't. Say "I love slow, sensual moments," or "If we could avoid anything involving exotic reptiles, that'd be swell." Your date isn't a mind reader, and you aren't Ms. Cleo (If you do not know who that is, I will wait again for you to Google).

4. **Laugh at the Absurdity:**

   Dating will present you with bizarre scenarios: someone bringing a plastic bag full of turkey hot dogs for "charity," an emoji bio that reads like a ransom note, or a Phil mix-up that requires CIA-level diplomatic skills to fix. When confronted with these absurdities, laugh. Humor is your secret weapon that turns disaster into a story you'll giggle about later. And trust me, your friends will thank you for the entertainment.

5. **Adjust Your Goals:**

   By now, you've realized that "The One" might be less about perfect compatibility and more about finding that special someone who can hold a decent conversation and will not flake like cheap mascara in the rain. Sometimes victory looks like meeting a person who just gets it—someone who, when faced with your quirks, responds with a smile instead of a grimace.

Here's the truth: The odds might not always be in your favor. The swiping math is grim, the bios are questionable, and half your dates feel like they came straight from a reality TV casting call. But you're still here, laughing, learning, and—most importantly—refusing to settle for anything less than what you deserve.

So go forth, dear reader. Enter the dating arena with confidence and clarity. Let your freak flag fly, communicate like a pro, set boundaries that would make a fortress jealous, and never forget to see the humor in it all. Because if love is a circus, you're the trapeze artist who swings with grace, the ringmaster who sets the stage, and the audience who knows exactly when to clap, cheer, and roll their eyes.

If all else fails, you've got stories—enough to fill a second or third book, enough to have your friends begging for updates at brunch. Consider this your permission slip to embrace the ridiculousness, cherish the surprises, and celebrate the fact that you're out there living, laughing, and loving on your own terms.

Epilogue: The Good, The Bad, and The Totally Forgettable

Well, folks, we've arrived at the grand finale of this dating circus, and what a ride it's been. I've swiped, typed, ghosted, been ghosted, and sampled every flavor of romance—from the shockingly awful to the unexpectedly wonderful, and even a few so utterly forgettable that my phone won't admit they existed.

For every swoon-worthy moment, I've had an equally cringe-worthy one—like that painfully awkward date where I almost faked an "emergency call" about my cat's raging fever. I've hurled my phone in frustration more times than I care to admit and scrolled through a sea of "Hey, how's it going?" texts that might as well have come from a half-asleep chatbot. Yet amid the digital disarray, I've stumbled on moments so unexpectedly sweet they made me swoon anyway. And yes, even as I wrote this, I was still waist-deep in dating disasters—a living reminder that the madness never really ends.

Dating is a full-contact sport, and I've got enough emotional bruises—and questionable text threads—to fill an ESPN highlights reel. Every "what the heck?" date and near-disastrous encounter is just another loop on the rollercoaster of romance. The upside? Each tragedy makes the triumphs shine like confetti cannons.

Case in point: once, a guy showed up to our first date in full scuba gear—flippers, wetsuit, the works—like he'd just escaped from a deep-sea documentary. Did I stay? Of course! My curiosity was doing backflips. Was there a second date? Let's just say I'm not ready to become a mermaid anytime soon.

Here's to the chaos, the awkwardness, and the occasional magic of modern dating. Keep swiping, my friends—and for the love of all that's good, leave the scuba suit at home.

Bonus Chapter
25 Ridiculous First Date Stories
(When Things Went Hilariously, Horribly Wrong)

Sometimes, first dates are magical. Other times, they're unforgettable for all the wrong reasons. So grab a drink, sit back, and let's dive into these 25 tales of first dates that went so sideways that they ended up in a whole different zip code. Buckle up!

1. **The Snake Charmer**

    He showed up to the date with his "emotional support" snake, Cleopatra, draped around his neck like a living scarf. "She's super chill," he assured me as her tongue flicked in my direction. I spent the evening pretending I was fine, but really, I was one wine spill away from screaming.

2. **The Roller-Skating Debacle**

    She suggested roller skating to "bring out our inner kids." Five minutes in, I hit the ground so hard I saw stars, and she was doubled over laughing. Then she fell on top of me. We left with matching bruises, but hey, at least we laughed through the pain.

3. **The Allergic Reaction to Romance**

    We went to a seafood restaurant, and he casually mentioned that he was allergic to shellfish. Apparently, "casually" wasn't strong enough because I ordered a shrimp cocktail and just being near it caused an instant reaction. They spent the next two hours with a swollen face and an EpiPen sticking out of their thigh.

4. **The Wife's Surprise Visit**

   Things were going well—too well. Midway through our second round of drinks, a woman stormed up to the table, threw a glass of wine in his face, and yelled, "Did you pay for this one too, Dan?" before storming out. He sheepishly shrugged and muttered, "It's... complicated."

5. **The Poetry Slam Gone Wrong**

   She invited me to a "casual poetry reading," which turned out to be her performing her own poetry... about her ex. It was four poems long, and I sat there, politely clapping as she angrily rhymed "pain" with "restrain."

6. **Mr. No Boundaries**

   He brought his mom. Enough said.

7. **The "Accidentally" Over-Intoxicated Date**

   She ordered margaritas like they were water, and I thought she could handle her liquor. By the time she was on her fifth, she was slurring her words and then sobbed uncontrollably because I "was too pretty to be on a date with her." I spent the rest of the date consoling her.

8. **The Gym Selfie King**

   He wore a tank top to dinner and spent 15 minutes showing me pictures of himself in different lighting. "The lighting is everything," he said, flexing under the table. I'd seen enough biceps for one lifetime.

9. **The Vomit Comet**

   We went to a theme park and got on one of those spinning rides. He was very braggadocios about his skills on coasters and threw up within seconds. The person on the other side of me threw up a minute later. I was covered in essentially a stranger's vomit. After we got off, we sat on a bench in shame and avoided eye contact for about 3 minutes, and I asked to be brought home.

10. The "Accidental" Blind Date

I showed up for what I thought was a date with an attractive, witty stranger. Turns out, it was my ex from five years ago who had catfished me. He called it "fate." I called it "stalking."

11. The Dog Dad

She showed up with her dog in a baby stroller and referred to it as her "child" all night. When I tried to pat it on the head, she scolded me for not asking permission first.

12. The Karate "Master"

He decided to impress me by showing off his "self-defense moves" in the parking lot. Long story short, he tried to do a high kick, slipped, and landed on his back. The ER nurse seemed unfazed by "first-date martial arts injuries."

13. The Crying Clown

She was in full face paint because she had "come straight from work." I didn't realize her job was being a clown. I tried to keep it together, but when she came back from the bathroom, she didn't get all of the white makeup off of her chin, and it looked like she had been pied in the face, and I laughed out loud.

14. The "Let's Get Matching Tattoos" Guy

We barely made it through appetizers when he suggested we get matching tattoos "for fun." I nervously laughed it off until he started Googling nearby tattoo shops.

15. The Liquor Enthusiast

He was way too excited to take me to his favorite whiskey bar, where he proceeded to give me an in-depth "tour" of every bottle on the wall. I pretended to care for the first hour, but by hour two, I was ready to drink the entire bottle myself.

16. The Breakup "Therapy" Date

She spent the entire evening talking about her ex and ended the date with, "Thank you so much—this was really therapeutic." Glad to be of service, I guess?

17. The Literal Cowboy

He showed up in full cowboy gear: hat, boots, belt buckle, and spurs. He insisted on ordering whiskey, and when they didn't have his brand, he muttered, "City folk…" and stormed out.

18. The Picnic Gone Wrong

She brought a cute picnic setup, complete with candles, which promptly attracted every bug within a ten-mile radius. I ended the date covered in mosquito bites and smelling like bug spray.

19. The Mushroom "Forager"

He ordered wild mushrooms at dinner and went on a rant about how much better they are when "harvested in the wild." Then he asked if I'd like to join him on a mushroom hunt. I kindly declined.

20. The Guy Who Tried to Teach Me to Salsa

He took me to a salsa bar and insisted on teaching me how to dance. After stepping on his foot for the fifth time, he exclaimed, "Are you even *trying*?" and left me on the dance floor alone.

21. The Doctor with a Weak Stomach

He was a med student who bragged about how "nothing grosses me out." But after a few cocktails, we hit the dancefloor, and a couple next to us got a little rowdy. He picked her up to spin her, and she landed hard on her ankle, and it looked broken. The bone was protruding, and when I told him that he should go look at it, he promptly passed out.

22. The Fishing Date Disaster

She insisted on taking me fishing, saying, "It's relaxing!" Two hours in, I accidentally dropped some of her expensive fishing lures in the lake. The rest of the date was spent lecturing me on the "sanctity of fishing equipment."

23. The Karaoke King

She picked a karaoke bar and insisted on singing every song. Every. Single. Song. At one point, she started serenading me with "Endless Love," and it was… endless.

24. The Guy who wore his Sponge Bob Pajamas

This man legit showed up in a blazer, a white tee, and silky sponge bob pajama pants. Enough Said.

25. The "Roommate" Who Was Clearly His Ex

Halfway through dinner, he admitted his "roommate" was his ex, who "just hasn't moved out yet." A quick glance at his phone showed her calling 11 times in a row. I didn't stick around to find out why.

And there you have it—25 reminders that, yes, dating is wild, unpredictable, and often straight-up ridiculous. Here's to the laughs, the weirdness, and the "Are you kidding me?" moments that make dating so memorable. May your own dates be less eventful... or at least provide a great story to tell at the next party. Cheers!

Made in the USA
Middletown, DE
29 May 2025